DO YOU KNOW THE
MUFFIN PAN?

100 Fun, Easy-to-Make Muffin Pan Meals

AMY FAZIO

Skyhorse Publishing

Skyhorse Publishing books may be purchased in bulk at special discounts for sales promotion, corporate gifts, fund-raising, or educational purposes. Special editions can also be created to specifications. For details, contact the Special Sales Department, Skyhorse Publishing, 307 West 36th Street, 11th Floor, New York, NY 10018 or info@skyhorsepublishing.com.

Skyhorse® and Skyhorse Publishing® are registered trademarks of Skyhorse Publishing, Inc.®, a Delaware corporation.

Visit our website at www.skyhorsepublishing.com.

10 9 8 7 6 5 4 3 2 1

Library of Congress Cataloging-in-Publication Data is available on file.

Cover photo credit: Amy Fazio

Print ISBN: 978-1-62914-693-5
Ebook ISBN: 978-1-62914-923-3

Printed in the United States of America

CONTENTS

INTRODUCTION:
"A MUFFIN PAN?"

"Really? You cook everything in your muffin pan? Like what?"

These are questions I heard a lot when I first started blogging in 2010. I was fascinated by the versatility of the muffin pan, how everything cooked in it held a unique shape and by the idea that I could make all my food portable. When I started my blog I was new to San Diego, unemployed, and had lots of time on my hands to browse the internet and create recipes to try out on unsuspecting neighbors and new friends. At this point the muffin pan had not caught on in the "food scene" quite yet, not like Brussels sprouts or biscoff cookies had. I continued to blog and research ways to cook in the muffin pan. The more exploring and writing I did, the more I heard people say "Oh, my family always uses the muffin pan to make meatloaf/cornbread/appetizers." The muffin pan was starting to gain popularity. I listened to suggestions from family members and friends on what they thought would make a great dish made in the muffin pan, plus some tried and true recipes they wanted to share.

Almost two years passed, I landed a teaching job, met a wonderful community of bloggers in San Diego, and began to hear people around me say "I saw a recipe online for a muffin pan cookie/egg nest/lasagna. Do you make those?"

And that was, coincidentally, right around the time I stopped blogging. My muffin pan had become vogue, like kale and cookie butter. I could not keep up with the demand of (finally) having a full time job *and* creating new recipes when so many talented people were trying the muffin pan out for themselves. I decided to give my muffin pan a rest.

Fast forward to the end of 2013. I was sitting in my classroom getting ready for my day when I received a text from a friend of mine that read "Hey Amy, would you be interested in writing a cookbook using the muffin pan?"

"Me? A cookbook?"
"You know I work fulltime, right?"
"I don't blog anymore, who would listen to me?"
"Wait, is this a joke?"

These were just some of the many questions that I was now asking. I told my friend I would need time to think about it but asked him to send me all the details. A cookbook . . . could I really do this? After I had tossed around all the possibilities of this daunting project in my head, over-thought every detail, calculated a budget, and booked a month long trip to Africa, I did what I always do when faced with a major life decision—I called my mama. And as the brilliant, caring woman that she is, she said without hesitation, "Of course you should write a cookbook. You'll be great. Just say yes."

And that is how, my dearest reader, we are here today. There were tears and triumphs, late nights and early mornings, full fridges and the occasional ice cream dinners, but I am so proud to say I've made it here. I truly hope you enjoy using this cookbook as much as I have enjoyed writing it. And remember:

"Just say yes, there's *muffin* to it!"

ESSENTIALS: TOOLS OF THE TRADE

MUFFIN PANS

In this cookbook the most important tool is, of course, the muffin pan. I use three different sizes:

Mini Muffin Pan, Standard Muffin Pan, and the Jumbo Muffin Pan.

I wanted to keep things simple. If you have different shaped pans such as loaf pans, tart pans, or heart-shaped pans, for example, use those. If you only have the standard pan, bake with that. I am a fan of using whatever you have on hand. Keep in mind some recipes may need some adjusting based on the shape of the pan. Bacon cups in a heart shaped pan would take a lot of work. (But if you pull it off, I want to see pictures!)

Mini Muffin Pan

This pan is primarily used for making appetizers or very small bites. With 12 or 24 wells per pan, this muffin pan is perfect for making many treats at once. Several of the recipes in this book can be adjusted to fit in the mini muffin pan.

Standard Muffin Pan

Often referred to as a regular pan or basic pan, this muffin pan comes with either 6 or 12 wells. Each well or cup holds a little more than ½ cup. This pan is the most versatile and widely used. The majority of the recipes in this book are made with this size pan.

Jumbo Muffin Pan

This pan is sometimes called a Texas muffin pan or large muffin pan. It is mainly used for making Texas sized muffins. In this book, it is most often used when making main dishes or edible bowls. Each Jumbo Muffin Pan normally has 6 large wells.

Silicone

Several recipes in this book call for a silicone pan. The advantage of silicone over the metal pans is their flexibility, which allows for easy removal. When I am making anything with chocolate or freezing a dish, silicone is my first choice.

WRAPPERS AND BINDERS

Wrappers are edible containers that line the wells of the muffin pan. They help ensure the smooth removal of the food while also playing an important role in the flavor of the dish. Wrappers can be placed open in the wells of the muffin pan, creating a cup or folded in, encasing the filling. If you flip the muffin pan over, wrappers can also be placed around the bottoms of the wells, creating edible dishes to hold delicious ingredients. Wrappers are not only impressive looking but functional as well.

Here is a list of my favorite and most used wrappers:

Bacon/Prosciutto
(Because I believe everything should be wrapped in bacon)
Puff Pastry
Phyllo
Biscuit Dough
Croissant Dough
Pizza Dough
Empanada Dough
Pie Crust
Wonton/Egg Roll Wrappers
Tortillas
Waffles
Noodles
Bread
Root Vegetables
(Thinly sliced and overlapped)

Binders are generally used when the dish has no wrapper. The most common binder used is egg. Eggs allow the dish to hold its shape while also giving it a fluffy, light texture. Another common binder is potatoes, or more specifically, the starch in potatoes. When cooked, the potatoes release the starch, which allows the dish to firm up and be removed easily from the pan. Just make sure to spray your pans well when cooking with potatoes. The final most common binder is cheese. Adding cheese won't always ensure easy removal, but when combined with a starch such as pasta, it makes a perfect little portion.

TOOLS OF THE TRADE:

Aside from the muffin pan, there are a few other tools I use quite often in the kitchen. This is a short list of my other favorite kitchen tools.

Cookie Scoop

Besides the muffin pans, the tool I use most often is an ice cream scoop. I bought it specifically for scooping cupcake batter uniformly into the muffin pan but I found it can be used for many other applications, such as cookie cup or savory batters. The cookie scoop will help ensure an even amount of food is distributed to every well of the muffin pan.

Round Cleaning Brush

Cleaning inside the muffin cups can be difficult. The round shape of the cleaning brush allows you to clean the cups with minimal effort.

Silpat

I wish everything could be covered in this silpat surface, especially my muffin pans. Nothing cooks up better and without sticking like the silpat.

Spouted Bowls

Many of the recipes call for a "spouted bowl" to make pouring ingredients into the small muffin cups easier. I have several different sizes of spouted bowls which are generally used for pouring eggs.

Paper Liners

Paper liners are handy if you are planning to bring a dish to share. Certain foods, like pastas and rice, will stick to the paper liners. Best used for bread based dishes like muffins or cornbread.

Hand-Held Blender

A hand-held or small counter top blender was invaluable during my recipe testing. The blender has several blade options such as whip or chop. It does the work of a food processor but on a smaller scale.

Frozen Garlic Cubes

I find these little garlic cubes to be the best time saver in the kitchen. They are stored in the freezer and whenever a recipe calls for garlic, I just pop one of the cubes out. Each cube is the equivalent to one clove. I have used other herbs such as crushed ginger and chopped basil and found I really like those as well.

MUFFIN PAN EQUATION

I have always been a much better cook than a baker. Honestly, the precision that baking the perfect biscuit takes has always been very daunting. It's not that I am bad at math or science, I am just truly left-brained. I like to be creative and make things. I love to experiment with food. Sometimes I make masterpieces. Sometime I make a mess. However, when I started writing this book I knew I needed to combine my love of being creative with being precise. There is a lot math and science that goes into cooking: Measurements, temperature, chemical reactions, etc. Through my recipe testing (and inevitable recipe mishaps) I have learned a lot about what can and cannot work in the muffin pan. I would love to say that if you mix something together, throw it in the muffin pan, and cook it up it will pop out perfectly every time. But, alas, I cannot. There is a science to making something work in the muffin pan. But have no fear! I have done the hard work for you and come up with an equation that should help turn almost any meal into a muffin pan meal!

Introducing the Muffin Pan Equations:

Muffin Pan + Wrapper + Filling
Muffin Pan + Binder + Filling
Muffin Pan + Filling + Freezer

Simple right? By adding together a muffin pan, some yummy ingredients, and something to keep it all together, you can create muffin pan masterpieces. Now, if you're anything like me you'd like some examples. So here are some simple ideas using the muffin pan equations that you can try any night of the week:

Jumbo Muffin Pan + 8-inch Flour Tortillas + Pinto Beans, Cheese & Diced Jalapeños =
Spicy Bean and Cheese Burrito Bowls, perfect for a quick lunch

Standard Pan + Eggs + cooked Quinoa & roasted veggie =
A healthy side dish, perfect with fish

Mini Silicon Pan + White Chocolate & Crushed Peppermint Candies + Freezer =
Last minute holiday dessert!

It's that easy. Almost every recipe in this book follows one of these three equations. It's the secret to my muffin pan success. For a list of some of the possible wrappers and binders, see previous section.

EMBRACE LEFTOVERS

In addition to being called "The Muffin Pan Lady," I am also a self-proclaimed Leftover Master Chef. I get it from my dad. As kids he used to make all kinds of creative dishes using leftovers or whatever we already on hand. A few memorable mornings he whipped up leftover Chinese food omelets. I know, I know, it's not for everyone but my dad loved them and loved making them. While I politely passed on the orange chicken with broccoli omelet, I did say yes to the creative pasta dishes and salads he thought up. From him I learned an appreciation for using leftovers in new and unexpected ways. That sense of creativity with food is what inspired me to start cooking in the muffin pan.

Some of my first muffin pan recipes were products of leftovers. One night I bought a whole cooked chicken for dinner. We had some simple black beans, Spanish rice, and corn tortillas to wrap it all up. The next day for lunch I shredded some of the chicken, mixed in a bit of beans and rice, added some cheese and a little enchilada sauce I had on hand and baked the mixture inside the tortillas. It made a great lunch and I only had to make just what I needed for me and saved the rest for some other meal.

While I worked hard to ensure the recipes measured out to exact numbers, some of these recipes will grace you with their own leftovers. For example, the recipe for Tomato Jewels with Whipped Feta and Herb Oil will most likely leave you with leftover whipped feta and herb oil. Embrace it! Grab a loaf of French bread and go to town or mix it all in with some fettuccini and call it dinner. It's going to be delicious because you made it. And even better, because no food was thrown away, our hard earned money was saved, and who doesn't love to save money?

Still not convinced of how wonderful the muffin pan is? Besides being just plain awesome, here are some reasons why you should consider using the muffin for your next meal.

- A great way to portion control your food.
- Perfect for cooking on a budget.
- Freezes easily for leftovers.
- Great for kids and toddlers.
- Easy to share or divide with others.
- Great for a grab and go lunch or snack.
- Clean-up is quick when everything is made in one pan.
- Great for turning almost any recipe into an appetizer.
- Shorter cook time so food is on the table faster.

Breakfast

BLUEBERRY FRENCH TOAST MUFFINS

Kids can learn a lot from working with adults in the kitchen. In this recipe, for example, young kids can count pieces of bread and blueberries to see how many can fit in each cup. Older kids can practice fractions by using measuring cups and measuring spoons. Fine motor skills are needed to crack eggs and gross motor skills are used to pour ingredients into bowls and stir. And then there is the all too important but toughest lesson of all, patience. Every step of the cooking process, even the clean up, can be educational. Yay for learning!

Pan: Standard 12-cup muffin pan

YOU WILL NEED:

Ingredients:

1 loaf of French bread, cut into small cubes
1 cup blueberries
6 eggs
2 cups of milk
½ cup sugar
1 tbsp vanilla extract

½ cup flour
½ cup brown sugar, packed
1 tsp cinnamon
¼ tsp nutmeg
¼ tsp salt
½ cup of cold butter, cut into pieces

Directions:

1. Spray a standard muffin pan.
2. Fill each cup with the cubed bread, 6 or 7 pieces. Place blueberries in a large measuring bowl. In mixing bowl with a pour spout, whisk together eggs milk, sugar, and vanilla. Pour the mixture over the bread cubes, pressing the bread down to absorb the liquid as you go. Continue to fill until all the liquid is distributed. It may look like there is too much liquid but keep pressing the bread and pouring. Cover the tray and refrigerate for 2 hours or overnight.
3. After the soaking period is complete, preheat the oven to 350°F.
4. Take the tray from the refrigerator and place blueberries on top.
5. In a mixing bowl, combine flour, brown sugar, cinnamon, nutmeg, and salt. Using your fingers or 2 forks, add the cold butter to the dry ingredients and crumble into coarse crumbs. Divide the topping among the cups.
6. Bake for 20-25 minutes, or until golden brown. Allow the muffins to rest for 5 minutes before serving.

Mix it Up: *You can soak the bread and egg mixture overnight in a shallow dish instead of the muffin pan. Then in the morning, mix in the blueberries and divide the whole bread mixture among the cups.*

EASY MEATY
BREAKFAST PIZZA BITES

"Did you say pizza for breakfast?" Yes I did! And not the cold variety from the night before but hot and fresh breakfast pizza made in the muffin pan.

Pan: 2 standard 12-cup muffin pans

YOU WILL NEED:

Ingredients:

6 uncooked sausage patties, quartered
4 slices bacon
2 red, green, or yellow bell peppers, diced

½ onion, chopped
5–6 eggs, beaten
1 cup mozzarella cheese, shredded
1 (11oz) roll of pizza dough

Directions:

1. Preheat oven to 400°F and grease a 12-cup muffin pan plus 2 cups from the second pan (14 cups in all).

2. In a large skillet, cook bacon until crisp. Place on a paper toweled plate to drain. Reserve a tablespoon of bacon fat to cook onions and peppers until tender. Finally, add pieces of sausage and cook until no longer pink. Place sausage on the plate with bacon.

3. Next, on a floured cutting board, roll out pizza dough. Cut pizza into 14 squares. Place one square in each cup.

4. Prebake the dough for 5 minutes. Remove pan from the oven and tamp the dough down using a tart shaper or the bottom of a shot glass.

5. Crumble bacon and add it, along with sausage, peppers, and onions evenly into each dough cup.

6. Fill each cup evenly with the eggs. Top each pizza cup with mozzarella cheese.

7. Bake for 8–10 minutes, or until the egg has set. If the cheese is browning too quickly, move the tray to the bottom rack and continue to cook.

MINI BRIE AND JAM PRETZEL BUNS

It's hard to go wrong with these ingredients together. The creaminess of the brie with the tangy raspberry and salty pretzel dough. Try and resist—I know I can't.

Pan: Standard 12-cup muffin pan

YOU WILL NEED:

Ingredients:

¼ lb brie, cut into cubes
Raspberry jam
1 ½ cups warm (105–110°F) water
1 tbsp granulated sugar
1 packet active dry yeast
4 ½ cups all purpose flour

2 tsp kosher salt
4 tbsp unsalted butter, melted
10 cups or 3 quarts of water
⅔ cup baking soda
1 egg yolk
1 tbsp water
Kosher or sea salt

Directions:

1. Combine water, sugar, and yeast in the bowl of a stand mixer; let sit 5 minutes until foamy.

2. Add flour, salt, and butter; stir to combine. Using a dough hook, knead dough on medium speed 5 minutes until smooth, elastic, and slightly tacky (alternatively, you can turn the dough out onto a lightly floured surface and knead by hand 10 minutes).

3. Shape dough into a ball and place in a large, lightly greased bowl. Cover with lightly greased plastic wrap and let rise in a warm place 1 hour until doubled.

4. When dough is nearly doubled, combine water and baking soda in a large stockpot. Bring to a boil. Heat oven to 400°F.

5. Punch down dough. Roll out on a lightly floured surface to ¼-inch thickness. Use a round biscuit or cookie cutter to cut out circles of dough. Re-roll out scraps as needed.

6. Spoon a tsp or so of jam into the center of half the dough circles. Top with a piece of brie. Top with another dough circle to form a pie; use fingers or fork tines to seal the edges. Transfer pies to a lightly floured baking sheet or platter.

7. Place about 3 buns at a time in the boiling water bath; boil 30 seconds. Using a slotted spoon, remove pies and transfer to the muffin cups. Repeat with remaining pies, placing one pie into each cup.

8. Lightly brush tops of buns with egg wash, then sprinkle with salt. Bake 12 to 14 minutes until golden brown and puffed. Cool slightly on a cooling rack before serving.

CARROT CAKE
PANCAKE MUFFINS

Part cake, part pancake, part muffin, all delicious. The muffin is simple to make and the cream cheese glaze really gives it that carrot cake taste.

Pan: Standard 12-cup muffin pan

YOU WILL NEED:

Ingredients:

2 cup flour
1 tsp baking soda
1 tsp baking powder
1 tsp cinnamon
¼ tsp salt
⅛ tsp fresh nutmeg
Dash of ground cloves
Dash of ground ginger

¼ cup brown sugar, packed
¾ cup buttermilk
1 tbsp canola oil
1 ½ tsp vanilla
2 eggs
¼ cup walnuts, chopped
1 ½ cup finely grated carrots
3 tbsp cream cheese
¼ cup powdered sugar
2 tbsp skim milk

Directions:

1. Preheat oven to 350°F and grease a standard 12-cup muffin pan.
2. In a mixing bowl, whisk together flour, baking soda, baking powder, spices, and salt.
3. In a separate bowl thoroughly combine sugar, buttermilk, oil, vanilla, and eggs. Add dry ingredients to wet ingredients and stir. Fold in walnuts and carrots.
4. Fill each cup ⅔ full. Bake for 15 minutes.
5. While the muffins are in the oven, prepare cream cheese glaze. Whisk together cream cheese, powdered sugar, and milk in a bowl. When the muffins are cooled enough to handle, dip the tops of the muffins in the glaze.

CHILAQUILES CASSEROLE CUPS

For over 25 summers, my family, along with two others, has vacationed together in Lake Tahoe. We stay in a great cabin, hang out by the lake, cook together, go rafting, swim, hit the casinos, and watch lots of movies. We are so fun, we call ourselves The HaHas. It suits us very well. The number of guests has grown over the 25 years but everyone who comes to stay is considered instant family. That's just how the HaHas are. One of my favorite parts of this trip is when we cook together. I have some talented cooks in this extended HaHa family, and many even have a signature dish. Judy makes desserts, Jill makes the salads, Chris mixes up cocktails, Joey barbecues, Mom makes blueberry pancakes, and Lupe makes the best chilequiles. Chilequiles are a combination of tortillas, enchilada sauce, onion, bacon and lots of love. I can't recreate the love she puts into her chilequiles but I did come up with a muffin pan version that I hope you enjoy. "Ha Ha."

Pan: Standard 12-cup muffin pan

YOU WILL NEED:

Ingredients:

12 corn tortillas, cut into pieces
4 slices of bacon, chopped
½ onion, chopped
7 oz can enchilada sauce, El Pato reccomended
2 cloves of garlic

2 cups of Mexican cheese blend, shredded
4 eggs
1 cup whole milk
1 tbsp garlic salt
⅛ tsp cumin
⅛ tsp oregano

Directions:

1. Preheat oven to 375°F and grease a standard muffin pan.

2. In a large frying pan over medium heat, cook bacon. Remove bacon to drain on a plate. Save fat that was rendered and cook onions until tender. Add tortillas and allow them to brown up a bit before adding enchilada sauce. Coat the tortillas in the sauce. Finally add the bacon back to the tortillas, stirring everything to coat before removing from heat.

3. In a bowl, mix eggs, milk, garlic salt, cumin, and oregano together.

4. Divide the tortilla mixture among the 12 cups. Cover the tops of the tortillas with cheese. Finally, pour the egg mixture over the tortillas.

5. Cook for 20 minutes. Serve with fresh salsa.

CROQUE MADAME IN A CROISSANT NEST

I knew I wanted to include a breakfast dish with a baked egg in this cookbook but I didn't want it to be your basic egg in toast or egg in phyllo. I wanted to get creative. So I did what any good researcher might do: I went out to breakfast. I perused the menu for inspiration and landed on a croque madam. Ham and cheese on a croissant topped with a béchamel sauce. Instantly I knew I had to try to put it in a muffin pan.

Pan: **Standard 12-cup muffin pan**

YOU WILL NEED:

Ingredients:
6 large croissants
12 pieces of ham, thinly sliced
1 cup grated gruyere
12 eggs
Dijon mustard

Béchamel Sauce
1 tbsp butter
2 tbsp flour
1 ½ cups whole milk
¼ cup parmesan, grated
A pinch of freshly grated nutmeg
Salt and pepper, to taste

Directions:

1. Preheat oven to 350°F and grease a standard 12-cup muffin pan.
2. Cut each croissant in half, lengthwise. Place one croissant half in each muffin cup.
3. On top of the croissant, layer a piece of ham, followed by a small dollop of mustard and finally crack an egg on top.
4. Place in oven and cook for 20 minutes.
5. While the egg cups bake, prepare the béchamel sauce. In a small sauce pan, melt butter over low heat. Using a wooden spoon, stir in flour. Slowly add milk and stir continuously until fully incorporated. Continue to stir until the sauce thickens and is smooth. Use a whisk to break apart any lumps. The finished sauce should be silky. Add grated cheese and stir until combined.
6. After the eggs have fully cooked, top the croissant cup with the béchamel sauce. Leftover sauce can be stored in the fridge for several days. Try it in lasagna!

EGG WHITE & TURKEY BACON CUPS

Bacon and eggs with a healthy twist. Still packed with flavor, this dish is a great make ahead breakfast to keep on hand.

Pan: **Standard 6-cup muffin pan**

YOU WILL NEED:

Ingredients:
6 slices turkey bacon
2 cup fresh spinach, washed
Clove of garlic, minced

3 sundried tomatoes, chopped
6 (or 1 ½ cups) egg whites
Feta, to taste

Directions:

1. Preheat oven to 350°F and grease a standard 6-cup muffin pan.

2. In a sauté pan, add sundried tomatoes, spinach and garlic. Sauté until spinach is cooked. Remove from heat.

3. Cut each strip of turkey bacon and place both pieces in an "X" in the muffin cup. Top the bacon with a tablespoon or so of the spinach tomato mixture. Add one egg white or a ¼ cup egg whites to each cup. Top with feta cheese.

4. Bake for 20 minutes, or until there is no more liquid on top of the egg whites.

EGGS BENEDICT CASSEROLE CUPS

I once had a conversation with a woman from room service about the benefits of hollandaise. I was young, given a menu to choose whatever I wanted and I landed on a dish called eggs Benedict. Has all the things I could possibly want except this weird sauce. "I'll have eggs Benedict but hold the sauce, please." The woman who was taking my order couldn't believe it. "But it's the best part! I'll put it on the side so you can try for yourself. Trust me, you'll like it." Turns out this pushy woman knew me better than I knew myself. Of course I loved the hollandaise. Now eggs Benedict is my favorite thing to order for breakfast.

Pan: Standard 12-Cup muffin pan

YOU WILL NEED:

Ingredients:
12 oz of Canadian bacon, diced
6 English Muffins, split and cut into cubes
4 eggs
1 cup whole milk
½ tsp onion powder
¼ tsp paprika

Hollandaise sauce:
3 large egg yolks
¼ tsp Dijon mustard
1 tsp fresh lemon juice
⅛ tsp cayenne pepper
½ tsp salt
⅛ tsp ground black pepper
½ cup unsalted butter, melted

Directions:

1. Grease a standard 12-cup muffin pan.
2. Fill each muffin cup with several bread cubes, pressing into the bottom. Sprinkle diced Canadian bacon among the cups. Fill all the space in each cup with the remaining bread cubes. They should be packed fairly tight.
3. In a mixing bowl, whisk eggs, milk and onion powder. Pour the mixture evenly over the 12 cups. Press the bread to help soak in the eggs. Continue to fill the cups until all the liquid is used.
4. Cover with foil and place in the refrigerator overnight.
5. The next morning, preheat the oven to 375°F.
6. Remove casserole cups from the refrigerator and uncover. Sprinkle paprika on top of the cups and return the foil.
7. Bake at 375°F, covered for 35 minutes. Uncover and bake for an additional 10-12 minutes, or until a knife, inserted in the middle, comes out clean.
8. Once the casserole cups are ready to serve, prepare the hollandaise.
9. In a blender, combine all egg yolks, mustard, lemon juice, cayenne, and pepper. Cover and blend until well combined, about 5 seconds.
10. Melt butter in a microwave safe spouted measuring cup for about 1 minute. With the blender on high speed, very slowly pour butter into the blender. The mixture will thicken quickly. Serve immediately.

HUEVOS RANCHEROS IN HOMEMADE CORN TORTILLAS CUPS

I can't say enough about how easy it is to make your own tortillas. I was nervous at first but I quickly got the hang of it. Using freshly made tortillas in this dish made it that much more delicious.

Pan: **Jumbo 6-cup muffin pan**

YOU WILL NEED:

Ingredients:

2 cups masa harina corn flour
1–2 cups hot water
½ tsp salt
1 cup refried beans
1 jalapeño, seeded and diced

⅔ cup cilantro, chopped
1 tsp ground cumin
½ cup shredded cheese (optional)
6 large eggs

Directions:

Tortillas

1. In a small bowl, dissolve salt in 1 cup of hot water. In a large bowl, add masa harina. Slowly pour salt water over the masa. Use your hands to mix the dough. Knead the dough for 2 minutes. Add water a tablespoon at a time to help reach the consistency of playdoh. It should feel smooth and slightly clammy to the touch. If the dough is too sticky it needs more masa. If the dough is crumbly add more hot water one tablespoon at a time.

2. Cover bowl with kitchen towel and allow to rest on the counter for 30 minutes to 2 hours. It is important to allow the dough to hydrate during this time.

3. When you are ready to work, begin by splitting the dough in half. Split each half in half again. Split the dough 2 more times until you have 16 even sized pieces.

4. Roll each piece into a ball and keep covered with kitchen towel. If the dough begins to dry out, dip your fingers into cold water before rolling the dough into a ball.

5. Using 2 large squares of parchment paper, place one piece of dough between the two sheets. Between a flat surface and a flat bottomed dish, like a casserole dish, frying pan, or flat dinner plate, press the center of the dough until flat and about ⅛ inch thick. You'll have to use those muscles to really get the tortillas flat. The tortillas should spread out to 6 inches in diameter. If the plates don't get the tortilla thin enough, continue with a rolling pin, moving from the center and rolling out toward the edges. Roll in varying directions to ensure it stays in a general circle shape.

6. Continue the process with the remaining balls of dough. Use a small piece of parchment paper between each tortilla if they are sticking together. Cover completed tortillas with another towel as you work.

7. Heat up large cast iron skillet over medium-high heat. Cook tortillas one at a time. Cook each side for 45 seconds to 1 minute each. The tortillas should puff as they cook on the second side. If the tortillas stiffen up, reduce the cook time to 40–45 seconds per side.

8. Adjust heat to medium if the tortillas become too crispy. Keep the cooked tortillas warm in the microwave or under a warm towel. The tortillas should stay flexible.

9. Repeat until all the dough has been cooked. Store in an airtight container in the refrigerator.

Huevos Rancheros

10. Preheat oven to 350°F and grease a jumbo 6-cup muffin pan.

11. If the tortillas were made ahead of time, microwave 6 tortillas covered in a damp paper towel at 30 second intervals until the tortillas are warm and flexible. Gently press 1 tortilla into each well.

12. In a bowl, mix together beans, jalapeños, cilantro, and cumin.

13. Add 1 tablespoon of beans to the tortillas. Top the beans with cheese and finally crack on egg into the cup.

14. Bake the dish uncovered for 25–27 minutes.

15. Serve with salsa and garnish with cilantro.

> **Tip:** *I prefer to put cheese under the eggs. When the cheese is on top, it makes it harder to see if the eggs are fully cooked. The cheese also creates a barrier that traps moisture, causing the eggs to require more cook time. To help ensure the yolk is in the center, crack the egg into a shallow bowl and slowly pour it on top of the bean and cheese.*

MINI ITALIAN BREAKFAST PIE

This dish has very few ingredients, very few steps, and that is just how I like it.

Pan: **2 standard 12-cup muffin pans**

YOU WILL NEED:

Ingredients:
4 slices of ham, quartered
4 slices of large genoa salami, quartered
2 roasted red peppers, drained and diced

1 can 8-count biscuits, split lengthwise
3–4 eggs
2 tbsp ricotta
Parmesan cheese, as a topping

Directions:

1. Preheat oven to 350°F and spray 16 cups of 2 standard muffin pans

2. Place one biscuit half in the well of the muffin cup and press firmly into the bottom. Layer one piece of ham and salami and several pieces of red pepper into each biscuit cup.

3. In a bowl, whisk together eggs and ricotta. Pour egg mixture on top of the meat evenly and very carefully. Sprinkle with parmesan cheese.

4. Bake for 15–17 minutes.

LIL' PEANUT BUTTER AND JELLY BREAD PUDDING

This recipe combines the peanut butter and jelly sandwich and bread pudding into one yummy breakfast treat. Add a glass of ice cold milk and you'll have some happy campers.

Pan: Standard 12-cup muffin pan

YOU WILL NEED:

Ingredients:
8 slices of white bread
½ cup of crunchy peanut butter
½ cup grape jelly
Butter

3 eggs
1 cup of cream
½ cup whole milk
¼ cup sugar
1 tsp vanilla extract

Directions:

1. Preheat oven to 350°F and grease a standard 12-cup muffin pan.
2. In a casserole dish large enough to hold the muffin pan, add 1 inch of water for a water bath. Place in the oven while the oven heats up.
3. Make 8 peanut butter and jelly sandwiches. Trim off the crusts. Butter both sides of the sandwich. With a sharp knife or pizza cutter, cut the sandwiches into cubes. Keep the cubes small enough to fit into the muffin pan. Fill the muffin cups with sandwich cubes until packed full.
4. In a spouted mixing bowl, whisk together eggs, cream, milk, sugar, and vanilla until fully incorporated.
5. Carefully pour the egg mixture over the pieces of bread. Push them down to soak up the liquid. Continue to pour until cups are full.
6. Allow the tray to soak on the counter for 5 minutes.
7. Place muffin pan in the water bath in the oven. Bake for 25 minutes.
8. Turn off the oven and very carefully remove just the muffin pan, leaving the dish of water to cool down.
9. Let the dish sit on the counter for another 5 minutes before serving.

Note: *For bread pudding, I find that thick white breads work best. Challah, brioche, french bread, and sourdough are among my favorites. Thick sliced bread, such as Texas toast also works really well.*

LOVE MUFFINS

I call these Love Muffins because both your children and your hips will love them!

Pan: **Standard 12-cup muffin pan**

YOU WILL NEED:

Ingredients:
2 ½ cups old fashioned oats
2 tbsp ground flax seed
1 cup plain low fat greek yogurt
2 eggs
½ cup honey

2 tsp baking powder
1 tsp baking soda
1 tsp vanilla extract
2 bananas, very ripe
½ cup dark chocolate chips
¼ cup walnuts, chopped

Directions:

1. Preheat oven to 350°F and spray a standard 12-cup muffin pan.

2. In a food processor, pulse oats for about 10 seconds. To the oats, add flax seed, yogurt, eggs, honey, baking powder, baking soda, vanilla, and bananas.

3. Mix in food processor until everything is well combined and smooth.

4. Take out the blade, carefully, and fold in chocolate chips and walnuts with spatula.

5. Divide the batter evenly among the 12 cups. Bake for 18–20 minutes or until a toothpick comes out clean.

6. Allow the muffins to cool on a rack before eating.

BUTTERNUT SQUASH CARAMELIZED ONION MINI QUICHE

This recipe highlights two of my absolute favorite ingredients: butternut squash and caramelized onions. The combination of the two is perfection. Paired with gorgonzola and baked up in a phyllo cup, these have become a staple in my brunch repertoire.

Pan: Standard 12-cup muffin pan

YOU WILL NEED:

Ingredients:

2 (12 oz) bags of chopped butternut squash or 4 medium butternut squash, peeled and cut into bite sized pieces
1 tbsp olive oil
Salt and pepper, to taste
1 tsp sugar
1 large yellow onion, chopped
1 tbsp butter
⅛ tsp baking soda
1 tsp salt

Pepper, to taste
¼ cup water
1 pkg phyllo dough, thawed as directed on package
Olive oil
1 cup half & half
3 eggs, lightly beaten
1 tbsp sage, thinly sliced
Salt & pepper, to taste
⅓ cup gorgonzola, crumbled

Directions:

1. Preheat oven to 350°F and spray muffin pan.
2. In a large bowl, toss butternut squash, oil, salt, and pepper until coated. Turn the squash out onto a greased baking sheet and bake for 30–40 minutes.
3. While the butternut squash bakes, prepare the caramelized onions.
4. In a skillet, over medium-high heat, heat sugar until melted and light brown, about 2 minutes. Add onions and stir with a wooden spoon until coated with sugar. Add butter, baking soda, salt and pepper. Stir onions and continue to cook until all the liquid is cooked out and there is a brown coating on the bottom of the pan, 6–8 minutes.
5. To deglaze the pan, add 1 tablespoon of water and scrape brown bits off the bottom of the pan. Stir occasionally until coating begins to appear again, after an additional 3 minutes. Add one more tablespoon of water and scrape the pan down again. Repeat this process, cooking for 3 minutes or so until coating forms, then add water and scrape down until all the water is used and onions are a rich deep brown color. Remove from the pan and allow to rest in a bowl at room temperature.
6. Check in on butternut squash. Give the tray a stir and return to the oven.

7. While the squash finishes cooking, prepare the phyllo cups. Brush oil between 6 sheets of phyllo. Cut the phyllo into 8 pieces, giving you 48 squares. Layer 4 squares of phyllo into each muffin cup, alternating the corners around the well of the muffin cup.

8. When the butternut squash has finished, remove from oven and pour into bowl with onions.

9. Mix together and spoon several pieces of the squash and onions into the phyllo cups. Divide cheese among the 12 cups.

10. In a spouted medium bowl, whisk together milk, eggs, sage, salt, and pepper. Carefully pour egg mixture on top of squash. Spray the tops of the phyllo with non-stick spray to help avoid burning.

11. Bake in 350°F oven for 15–20 minutes.

BANANA-NUT
MONKEY BREAD MUFFINS

This is a very kid friendly recipe. The name monkey bread makes it fun, the small pieces of bread make it perfect for those tiny toddler hands, and the combination of peanut butter and bananas just makes it delicious.

Pan: Standard 12-cup muffin pan

YOU WILL NEED:

Ingredients:
1 can (16.3 oz.) refrigerated but-
    termilk biscuits, each cut into
    quarters
1 small banana, coarsely chopped
6 tbsp peanuts, divided

1 cup brown sugar
¼ cup butter, melted
2 tbsp creamy peanut butter
1 tbsp water
¼ cup granulated sugar
1 ½ tsp cinnamon

Directions:

1. Preheat oven to 350°F and grease a 12-cup muffin pan.

2. Divide the banana pieces along the bottom of the muffin cups. Sprinkle ¼ cup of the peanuts on top of the bananas.

3. In a microwave safe bowl, combine brown sugar, butter, peanut butter, and water. Heat on high for 1 minute or until butter is melted. Stir and pour over bananas and nuts.

4. In a food processor, pulse the remaining nuts, sugar, and cinnamon until nuts are ground fine. Pour into shallow dish. Roll the dough pieces in the sugar mixture. Place 4–6 dough pieces into each cup. Press dough into the bottom firmly.

5. Bake for 15 minutes or until golden brown.

6. To remove muffins from the pan, loosen the edges with a butter knife. Place a baking tray on top of the pan, holding firmly, and invert the muffins on to the tray.

BREAKFAST POLENTA CUPS

Start your day right with these creamy hearty polenta cups.

Pan: **Standard 6-cup muffin pan**

YOU WILL NEED:

Ingredients:

12 oz precooked polenta cubed
2–3 tbsp heavy cream or milk
1 (8 oz) slab of creamy blue Brie
    Cheese, cubed

1 tbsp rosemary, minced
½ cup parmesan cheese
Salt and pepper, to taste
6 eggs

Directions:

1. Preheat the oven to 350°F and spray 6 wells of a standard muffin pan.

2. Place the cubed polenta in a microwave safe dish and heat for 2 minutes. Add rosemary and smash polenta with a fork. Add cream to the polenta and stir. Add another tablespoon if the mixture appears too clumpy.

3. Pour polenta into the muffin pan and press into the center to create a well. Place one cube of creamy cheese into the well.

4. In a small bowl, carefully break one egg. Pour the egg from the bowl into the cup, doing your best to place the egg on top of the cheese.

5. Bake the dish for 10 minutes. Take out of the oven and cover egg in parmesan cheese.

6. Bake for an additional 5 minutes, or until egg has set.

EGG MUFFINS

Great for breakfast on the go. This egg muffin is a take on the classic Italian sausage and peppers sandwich.

Pan: **Standard 12-cup muffin pan**

YOU WILL NEED:

Ingredients:
6 whole English muffins, split into 12 halves
½ lb Italian sausage, ground
1 bell pepper, chopped
¼ cup mozzarella cheese, shredded
6 large eggs
¼ cup milk
1 tsp Italian seasonings
Salt and pepper, to taste

Directions:

1. Preheat oven to 375°F and spray a standard muffin pan.
2. Prepare muffin pan by placing one half of an English muffin into each cup. Using a tart shaper or shot glass, press the English muffin into the bottom of the cup.
3. In a skillet, break sausage into large chunks and brown for 5 minutes, or until no longer pink. Stir in peppers and cook for an additional minute. Remove from heat and divide sausage and peppers among the muffin cups. Top the sausage and peppers with shredded cheese.
4. In a spouted bowl, whisk together eggs, milk, Italian seasonings, salt and pepper. Carefully pour the egg mixture over sausage, peppers, and cheese.
5. Bake for 15–17 minutes, until a knife inserted in the cup comes out clean.

Note: *This dish is very versatile. You can use sweet, mild, or spicy sausage. Also, broccoli works well in place of peppers. Finally, mozzarella can be substituted for any shredded cheese you have on hand.*

MINI CARNE ASADA FRITTATAS WITH SWEET POTATO CRUST

I adore the sweet potato crust on these mini frittatas. They take a little work but it is worth the effort.

Pan: **Standard 12-cup muffin pan**

YOU WILL NEED:

Ingredients:
2–3 sweet potatoes, peeled and sliced very thin
14 oz carne asada steak, diced
½ cup onion
½ cup red bell pepper
1 cup mushrooms, washed and chopped
6 eggs
½ cup milk
¼ cotija cheese, crumbled
Salt and pepper

Directions:

1. Preheat oven to 400°F and spray a standard muffin pan very well.

2. In each muffin cup, layer 2 or 3 sweet potato slices to cover bottom. Stand additional 3 or 4 slices around the edge of the muffin cup, overlapping to help ensure they stay standing. If the potato slices are falling over, place a ball of foil into each cup.

3. Bake the sweet potato crust at 400°F for 15 minutes.

4. Meanwhile, in a large skillet, heat a tablespoon of oil over medium heat. Cook onions, peppers, and mushrooms for 3–4 minutes, then add steak. Continue to cook until steak is cooked through and veggies are tender. Should only take another minute or two.

5. When the crust has finished prebaking, remove from oven. Then lower oven to 375°F.

6. Divide the steak and mushroom mixture among the sweet potato crusts. Adjust the sweet potato slices if they have fallen.

7. In a spouted bowl, whisk together eggs, milk, cotija, salt, and pepper. Carefully pour the egg mixture over steak.

8. Bake at 375°F for 18–20 minutes, or until a sharp knife comes out cleanly.

WILD MUSHROOM LEEK AND GOAT CHEESE EGGS IN PROSCIUTTO BASKETS

True, it is another egg in a nest recipe but this time loaded up with delicious leeks, wild mushrooms, and creamy goat cheese. Then to make it even better, it is wrapped in delicious prosciutto.

***Pan:* Standard 6-cup muffin pan**

YOU WILL NEED:

Ingredients:
8–10 slices of prosciutto
6 eggs
1 cup mushrooms, washed and chopped
1 small leek whites, quartered and sliced thin

2 tbsp goat cheese
1 clove garlic
Fresh parsley
Salt and pepper, to taste

Directions:

1. Preheat oven to 350°F and lightly grease a standard muffin pan.

2. In a large skillet, heat 1 tablespoon of oil over medium heat. Cook mushrooms and leeks for 2 minutes, seasoning with salt and pepper to taste. Add in garlic and continue to cook for 5–6 minutes, stirring occasionally. Set aside.

3. Line the inside of each muffin cup with a slice of prosciutto, creating a cup. Tear the extra slices of prosciutto in pieces and divide among the cups to make sure the bottoms of the cups are covered.

4. Scoop the mushroom and leeks into the prosciutto cups, about 1 heaping tablespoon. Add 1 tsp of goat cheese. Press down with a spoon to make room for the egg. Finally, crack an egg into each cup.

5. Bake for 18–20 minutes for a soft yolk, 20–25 minutes for a firm yolk. Place on a rack and allow to rest for 5 minutes before serving.

APPLE CINNAMON OATMEAL CAKES

These oatmeal cakes are great for a grab and go breakfast. All the comfort and warmth of oatmeal on the go.

Pan: **Standard 12-cup muffin pan**

YOU WILL NEED:

Ingredients:

2 cups rolled oats
¼ cup brown sugar, packed
1 tsp baking powder
1 ½ tsp cinnamon
¼ tsp salt
½ cup egg whites or 1 whole egg

1½ cup milk, any variety and combination
   (I used 1 cup 2% milk and ½ cup
   coconut milk)
¼ cup unsweetened applesauce
1 apple, peeled and chopped into ½" pieces
½ cup raisins
¼ cup walnuts, chopped

Directions:

1. Preheat oven to 350°F and spray standard muffin pan.
2. In a large bowl combine oats, brown sugar, baking powder, cinnamon, and salt.
3. In a separate bowl, whisk together egg, milk, and applesauce.
4. Add wet ingredients to the dry ingredients and mix thoroughly.
5. Fold in apple, raisins, and nuts.
6. Fill each cup with the oatmeal mixture.
7. Bake for 25–30 minutes, or until the tops are golden brown.
8. After removing from the oven, let the cakes cool for 10 minutes before removing from the pan.

DUTCH BABY BOWLS WITH COUNTRY SAUSAGE

I'm pretty positive my love for brunch comes from my mother (and not just because of our shared love for mimosas). Growing up we had a lot of family living near by and on Sundays we would get together for brunch. My mom would make the best food. There are two dishes that stand out the most for me: Dutch Babies and Country Sausage Pie. I used to ask my mom to make "the baby thing with the butter" and because she's a mom, she knew exactly what I meant. Several years and more teeth later, she made us country sausage pie and I was hooked on brunch. Now many more years have passed, and I have the honor of combining these two memorable dishes into one muffin pan brunch dish for you all, in honor of my mother and all her hard work in the kitchen. I raise my mimosa to you, Mama.

Pan: 2 standard 12-cup muffin pans

YOU WILL NEED:

Ingredients:

1 cup milk
6 eggs
1 cup flour
⅛ tsp salt
¼ cup unsalted butter, melted
3 Italian sausage links

½ apple, peeled and diced
¼ cup raisins
1 potato, baked, cooled, and diced
½ yellow onion, diced
½ tsp dried sage
⅛ tsp cinnamon
Salt and pepper, to taste

Directions:

1. Preheat oven to 400°F and spray 2 standard muffins pans.

2. In a blender, mix together milk, eggs, flour, and salt until well blended. If the butter is still warm, let it get to room temperature before pouring it into the blender. This will ensure the hot butter doesn't cook the eggs.

3. Divide the batter evenly among the 24 cups, filling each cup halfway full.

4. Bake at 400°F for 13–15 minutes. They will expand while they bake, like a popover, but will settle and sink when taken out of the oven.

5. While the dutch babies bake, prepare the country sausage filling.

6. In a skillet over medium heat, brown the sausage links for 2–3 minutes. They do not need to be fully cooked, just firm enough to be sliced. Remove the sausage and slice into rounds. (If you are using fully cooked sausage, you can skip this step and slice the sausages before adding them to the pan.) Return the sausage to the pan. Mix in the apples, raisins, potatoes, onions, sage, and cinnamon. Add salt and pepper to taste.

7. Remove from the heat when the onions are softened and sausage is no longer pink.

8. Serve the sausage mixture in the dutch baby cups.

Appetizers

MY CHEDDAR, APPLE, SAUSAGE BISCUITS

This recipe gets the very special title of "My" because out of all the recipes in this book, I may be most proud of this one. This was the first recipe I wrote back on my blog in 2010, and was created entirely from what I had on hand. The sausage and biscuit make it a hearty appetizer while the apple, cheddar, and hint of rosemary give it some class. It's a crowd pleaser.

Pan: 2 standard 12-cup muffin pans, nonstick

YOU WILL NEED:

Ingredients:
1 can refrigerated biscuits
½ package
½ lb ground Italian
   sausage

½ cup cheddar cheese, grated
1 med yellow onion, chopped
1 large red apple, chopped
1-2 tbsp rosemary, chopped
Salt and pepper to taste

Directions:

1. Preheat the oven to 375°F.

2. Add the sausage to the skillet on medium heat, breaking it apart with a spatula. Cook sausage for a minute or two. Throw in the apples and onions. Cook until meat is no longer pink and onions are softened. Turn off the heat and salt to taste.

3. Grease two non-stick muffin pans. If you are using a biscuit with added butter flavor, there is no need to grease the pans. Slice each biscuit lengthwise. You should have 16 slices in total. Place each slice of biscuit in the well of muffin pan. Use a spoon or the end of a shot glass to get the biscuit in there nice and snug.

4. Spoon the sausage, apple, onion mixture into each biscuit cup. Add a pinch of the rosemary to each cup and top with a sprinkle of the cheddar cheese.

5. Bake for 18 minutes or until the edges begin to turn golden brown. Remove and serve immediately.

SOUTHWEST EGGROLL BUNDLES WITH CHIPOTLE CREAM SAUCE

While writing this cookbook I brought most of my recipes into work. It was great not having all that food in my fridge. It was also nice having my coworkers try the food and let me know what they thought. Built-in taste testers. This one got a lot of great reviews and even some next day "Those eggroll cups you made yesterday were so good!" and "That dipping sauce really made the dish!" And I'd have to agree with them. These are great and the dipping sauce does make this dish stand out.

Pan: **Standard 12-cup muffin pans**

YOU WILL NEED:

Ingredients:
1–2 tbsp vegetable oil
1 cup red bell pepper, chopped
½ cup green onion, chopped
1 cup black beans, drained and rinsed
1 ½ cup frozen corn
1 whole jalapeño, seeded and diced
2 large chicken breast, cooked and diced
2 tsp cumin
2 tsp chili powder
1 tsp cayenne

1 ½ cup Monterey Jack cheese, shredded
12 egg roll wrappers

Dipping Sauce:
½ cup of cream cheese, softened
1 chipotle pepper in adobo sauce, seeded and minced
1 tbsp adobo sauce, from the jar
2 tbsp fresh lime juice
2–3 tbsp milk, cream, or half & half, or broth for thinning
Salt, to taste

Directions:

1. Preheat oven to 350°F and grease a standard muffin pan.

2. In a large skillet, sauté bell pepper and green onion in oil for 3–5 minutes, or until soft. Next, add the black beans, frozen corn and jalapeño to the pan and cook until heated through. Finally, add the chicken, cumin, chili, cayenne, and salt. Stir until combined. Remove the pan from the heat and stir in the cheese.

3. To fill egg rolls, very gently place press one wrapper in each well of the muffin pan. Spoon the mixture, about 2 tablespoons or half full, into each cup. Bring the four corners to the middle to form a peak. Pinch the corners together and twist the top tightly. Use water to help seal the edges.

4. Place the muffin pan on the lowest rack and set the timer for 22 minutes.

5. While the eggrolls are baking up, gather the ingredients to mix up the dipping sauce. Mix all the ingredients together, thinning out with the milk until you reach the desired consistency.

6. Check on the eggrolls, making sure the peaks do not become too brown. When they reach a nice golden brown, remove from the oven.

7. Allow the cups to cool for a minute before removing from the pan. Make sure the bottoms have began to crisp up. If not, they may need a minute or two back in the oven to firm up. Once they seem firm, remove all the eggroll cups from the pan and allow to cool. This will further harden the eggroll wrapper.

8. The egg rolls can be served warm or cold with the dipping sauce.

CREAMY CHICKEN CORDON BLEU BUNDLES

This already classic French dish gets another layer of decadence with the addition of creamy French brie. While these make for a great appetizer, you can also serve two of these bundles with a nice green salad and call it lunch/ dinner. Bon appétit!

Pan: **2 Standard 12-cup muffin pans**

YOU WILL NEED:

Ingredients:
1 box (2 sheets) of Puff Pastry
2 chicken breasts, boneless skinless, about 1 lb total
1 tbsp ground mustard
1 tbsp garlic salt

20 slices of ham
¼ lb brie, cut into 18 cubes
1 cup swiss or gruyere cheese, shredded
½–1 cup water, or other cooking liquid (such as broth or wine)

Directions:

1. Preheat oven to 400°F and grease 18 cups of two standard muffin pans.

2. In a pan large enough to hold the chicken and liquid comfortably, add the two chicken breasts and cover with cooking liquid. I use water in this case but you can use broth, white wine, cider, beer, or a combination of whatever suits your fancy. Add enough cooking liquid to cover the chicken. To the liquid, add the ground mustard and garlic salt. Bring to a boil at medium-high heat, then bring the heat to low and cover. Cook until chicken is no longer pink, about 10–15 minutes depending on the thickness of the chicken.

3. When the chicken is all cooked, pour out the liquid, and dice the chicken into cubes. Prepare the ham as well. Stack several pieces of ham and cut into quarters.

4. Only when everything else has been prepped, take the puff pastry from the refrigerator. On a lightly floured surface, roll out the first sheet. Keep the second sheet in the fridge. Keeping the puff pastry cold ensures maximum puff when baked.

5. Cut each pastry sheet into 9 pieces, 3 across and 3 down. Place the puff pastry squares into each muffin cup.

6. First layer to go into the cup is ham, pushed in gently. Next layer is several cubes of chicken, followed by a cube of brie. Lastly cover each cup with a generous amount of shredded cheese. Repeat with the second sheet of pastry and muffin pan.

7. Bake for 10–12 minutes. The outside should be just turning light brown.

Note: *This dish is fabulous on its own or served with a nice French mustard for dipping. Other sandwiches such as a Cuban or a Muffaletta would work well here too.*

CRANBERRY BRIE BUNDLES WITH TOASTED PISTACHIOS

Festive, and oh-so-simple to make, this recipe is sure to be a crowd pleaser at any holiday party.

Pan: **Mini 24-cup muffin pan**

YOU WILL NEED:

Ingredients:
24 Wonton Wrappers
8 oz Brie Cheese, cut into ½ inch
  cubes

½ cup dried cranberries, chopped
½ cup pistachios, shelled and
  coarsely chopped
2–3 green onions, whites only,
  chopped

Directions:

1. Preheat oven to 375°F and grease the pan.

2. Heat a skillet over medium heat and add pistachios. Toast for a minute or until just golden brown and fragrant.

3. Place wonton wrapper in the well of each mini muffin cup. Into each cup add one cube of brie. Evenly distribute pistachios, then green onions, and finally cranberries among the 24 cups.

4. Your Choice: You can leave the wonton wrapper open like a blossom or close up the ends in a star shape.

5. Bake at 375°F for 7–8 minutes, until cheese is melted and edges begin to brown. This dish is best served warm.

Mix It Up: *Try this bold variation! The amounts and directions are the same.*
Blue brie (such as Cambozola) · Dried cherries · Toasted walnuts · 1 shallot, chopped and caramelized

HOT PEPPER JELLY AND CREAM CHEESE STARS

For a person whose medium is the muffin pan, who has never tried to make jelly or jam in her life, I seriously impressed myself with this recipe. After patting myself on the back, I mixed the jelly with some cream cheese, wrapped it in a wonton, and impressed myself again.

Pan: **Mini 24-cup muffin pan**

YOU WILL NEED:

Ingredients:
24 Wonton Wrappers
Cream Cheese

Hot Pepper Jelly
1 red bell pepper, seeded and diced
1 jalapeño, seeded and diced
1 small Santa Fe pepper, with seeds, diced
1 ½ cup apple cider vinegar, divided
4 cups sugar
1 (3 oz) pouch of liquid pectin (I use Certo)

Directions:

1. Set the oven for 375°F.

2. Combine diced peppers and half cup of the apple cider vinegar in a blender or food processor for several pulses. This will mince up the peppers to eliminate the need to strain later.

3. In a 6-quart sauce pan, combine the blended pepper mixture, the rest of the vinegar, and sugar. Bring to a rolling boil on high heat, stirring continuously.

4. Remove the pan from the heat and stir in the liquid pectin. Ladle jelly into jars. Follow the directions on the package of pectin if you would like to sanitize and store the jars.

5. Allow several minutes for the jelly to set.

6. Prepare your mini muffin pan by very lightly spraying the wells with cooking spray. Place one wonton or pot sticker wrapper into each cup. Place approximately 1 tsp each of hot pepper jelly and cream cheese into the wrapper.

7. Using a little bit of water to help seal the edges, pinch two opposite sides together. Bring the remaining two side towards the middle and pinch. Use as much water as needed to seal edges into a star shape.

8. Bake at 375°F for 13–15 minutes or until the wrappers are light brown. Remove the wontons from the pan immediately to cool on a rack.

EDAMAME
WALNUT BLOSSOMS

The combination of the wine, garlic, and walnuts served up in won ton cups makes this a very flavorful and elegant appetizer.

Pan: Mini 24-cup muffin pan

YOU WILL NEED:

Ingredients:

1 ½ cups of edamame, shelled
⅓ cup of walnuts, finely chopped
Olive oil
½ an onion, diced

1 tsp of brown sugar
2 garlic cloves, minced
⅓ cup of white wine
1 package of wonton wrappers
Salt and pepper to taste

Directions:

1. Preheat oven to 375°F and grease the mini muffin pan.

2. Heat a medium skillet over medium heat with 1–2 tablespoon(s) of olive oil. Add onions and cook until translucent. Next, add the sugar and continue to cook until the onions begin to caramelize. Remove from the heat and put the onions aside.

3. Place the same pan back on the heat and add the walnuts and toast until they just begin to brown. Once they begin to brown, add the edamame, garlic, white wine, the caramelized onions back in the pan, and season with a generous amount of salt and pepper.

4. Continue to cook until the white wine begins to bubble and evaporate.

5. *Your Choice:* You can add the mixture to the food processer and blend it for a creamy filling or place the mixture in a bowl and smash with a fork for a crunchy texture.

6. In the greased muffin pan place one wonton wrapper into each of the 24 cups. Place a tablespoon of the mixture into each wonton wrapper. Spray the edges of the wonton wrappers with olive oil spray to avoid burning.

7. Cook at 375°F for 12 minutes, or until the wonton wrapper begins to brown. Serve warm.

Note: *If you are making this dish for vegan friends, you can replace the wonton wrappers with phyllo dough.*

FRENCH ONION SOUP DUMPLINGS

I love San Diego. It's almost always sunny and very rarely do we have cold days, or at least the kind the rest of the country would call "cold." I admit, occasionally I miss those chilly, gray, rainy days. The kind where you lay in bed watching movies, sipping hot soup and pretending you had grand plans for the day, like "I would be out running that half marathon today and painting the house if it weren't for this rain." Much to my delight, while working on this cookbook, Southern California finally had some much needed rain. So I mixed up a batch of these warm soup dumplings, expressed my disappointment to my cat about how I was bummed that I couldn't climb the mountain I planned on conquering that day, and settled in for a Harry Potter marathon.

Pan: Mini 24-cup muffin pan

YOU WILL NEED:

Ingredients:

1 tbsp olive oil
3 tbsp unsalted butter
1 tsp or 1 clove of garlic, minced
1 large yellow onion, sliced thinly
1 tsp fresh thyme leaves

Salt and pepper to taste
1 tsp sugar
3 tbsp beef broth
1 sheet 9x9 puff pastry
Whole grain mustard
⅓ cup grated gruyere or Swiss cheese

Directions:

1. Preheat oven to 400°F.
2. Over medium heat, add oil and butter to a heavy bottom pan, preferably cast iron if you have it, and stir until melted. Add the onions and garlic to the pan and stir to coat them. Leave the onions in the dish for several minutes, undisturbed.
3. Turn down the heat to medium low and add the sugar, thyme, salt, and pepper and give the onions another stir. Continue stirring every so often to ensure the onions don't burn. The whole process takes about 30–40 minutes.
4. When the onions are all browned and soft add the beef broth and deglaze the pan. Use a wooden spoon to scrape any bits that are stuck to the bottom.
5. Remove pan from heat and let it rest while you prepare the puff pastry. On a lightly floured surface, unfold the thawed puff pastry and cut into 24 squares. A pizza cutter works well here. I prefer to cut the dough into 6 slices first then across each slice 4 times to create the 24 squares.
6. Place a square into each cup. Add a small spread of mustard, next adding a spoonful of the onions, finally topped by a generous amount of cheese. Fold the corners into the middle.
7. Bake for 12 minutes or until puffed and golden brown. Remove from the oven and allow to cool before serving. This recipe does very well at room temperature.

Note: *This recipe is a great one to freeze and have in your arsenal when you need to whip up a last minute appetizer. They can be baked frozen or thawed. Add 3–5 minutes if baked directly out of the freezer.*

PETITE GORGONZOLA CHEESECAKE WITH A WALNUT CRUST

I first had gorgonzola cheesecake at a restaurant here in San Diego. It was offered on the dessert menu and everyone at the table was curious about it. We ordered it and loved it! When we told the waiter how much we had enjoyed it, even though it seemed scary he suggested trying it out next time as an appetizer. Boy was he right. I was inspired by that cheesecake to make my own version, served as an appetizer.

Pan: **Mini 24-cup muffin pan**

YOU WILL NEED:

Ingredients:

½ cup walnuts
¼ cup panko bread crumbs
3 tbsp butter, melted
¼ cup sugar
1 egg white

1 egg
8 oz cream cheese
4 oz Gorgonzola cheese
1 cup candied walnuts
½ pear, diced
Honey

Directions:

1. Preheat oven to 350°F and spray a mini muffin pan.

2. In a food processor, finely chop walnuts. To the walnuts, add bread crumbs, melted butter, and egg white and mix. Add a tsp of crust mixture to each muffin cup. Using a tamp or just your thumb, press the crust down firmly.

3. Bake the crust for 5 minutes.

4. While the crust bakes, heat the cream cheese and gorgonzola in a microwave safe bowl for 2–3 minutes. Stir the mixture until smooth. When the cream cheese mixture is cool, whisk in egg.

5. Divide the cream cheese mixture among the 24 muffin cups.

6. Bake the cheesecake for 15 minutes, or until light brown and puffed.

7. When done, allow the cheesecake to cool. When ready to serve, top each cheesecake bite with a piece of pear and drizzle of honey.

IRISH NACHO STACKS

All the beauty of Irish Nachos stacked up in the muffin pan.

Pan: Standard 12-cup muffin pan

YOU WILL NEED:

Ingredients:

½ cup panko bread crumbs
1 tbsp unsalted butter, softened
2 lbs russet potatoes, peeled and sliced
1 ¼ cup half and half
1 ¼ tsp salt
¾ tsp pepper
1 ⅓ cup Irish white cheddar, shredded
⅔ cup Parmesan cheese, grated
2 tsp cornstarch
1 jalapeño, seeded and diced
½ cup of cooked bacon, crumbled
Pico de gallo
Sour cream

Directions:

1. Preheat oven to 425°F, move oven rack to lowest position, and grease a standard muffin pan with butter.

2. Pulse panko crumbs in a food processor until finely ground and press ground panko into the sides of the cup.

3. In a large microwave safe bowl, combine potatoes, half & half, salt and pepper. Cover the bowl with plastic wrap and microwave for 12–15 minutes, just until tender. Stir once halfway through.

4. While the potatoes are in the microwave, in a separate bowl, combine cheddar, parmesan, and cornstarch. Scoop ⅓ cup of the mixture and reserve for a topping.

5. When the potatoes are done, add the jalapeño and bacon and gently stir. To that, add the remaining cheese mixture to the bowl and stir again until smooth. Evenly divide the potato mixture among the 12 cups. Top with the reserved cheese.

6. Spray the underside of a large piece of foil with cooking spray. Cover the potatoes, greased side down.

7. Bake for 10 minutes. Remove foil and bake for an additional 13–15 minutes, or until golden brown.

8. Run a knife around the potato cup. Allow to cool in the muffin pan. Turn potatoes out onto a serving tray. Allow to cool for additional 5 minutes.

9. Serve with pico de gallo and sour cream.

PANCETTA MUSHROOM TASSIE

Tassies are traditionally served as a dessert and filled with pecans or lemon curd. I don't really have much of a sweet tooth to speak of, so I put pancetta and mushrooms in my tassies and serve them as an appetizer instead.

Pan: **Mini 24-cup muffin pan**

YOU WILL NEED:

Ingredients:

4 oz pancetta, diced
½ cup mushrooms, cleaned and chopped
4 oz (8 tbsp) unsalted butter
4 oz cream cheese
1 ½ cup all-purpose flour

½ cup half & half
1 large egg
⅛ tsp salt
½ cup grated parmesan cheese
¼ cup chopped fresh chives
Cayenne pepper to taste

Directions:

1. Preheat oven to 375°F and spray a 24 mini muffin pan.

2. In a stand mixer fitted with the paddle attachment, cream the butter and cream cheese. On low speed, gradually add flour. Once the mixture has combined, divide mixture into 24 balls and place on a lined baking sheet in the refrigerator for an hour.

3. While the dough chills, cook pancetta and mushrooms in a medium skillet. Fry pancetta until fat is rendered and the mushrooms are cooked, about 6-7 minutes. Drain the mushroom and pancetta in a fine mesh sieve or on a paper toweled plate.

4. Take dough from the refrigerator and place one ball in each cup. Press the dough in the center with your thumb, pressing the dough into the sides, creating a well in the center of the dough.

5. In a bowl, whisk together egg, half & half, and salt. Divide the pancetta and mushroom mixture into each dough cup. Top with a tsp or so of Parmesan.

6. Carefully pour the egg mixture into the remaining space on top of the cheese.

7. Bake for 20 minutes or until puffed and golden brown.

8. Allow the tassies to cool on a rack before serving.

Note: *Cooled leftovers can be stored in an airtight container in the refrigerator for up to 3 days. Reheat in a 350ºF oven for 5–10 minutes or until warmed through.*

PRETZEL DOG DIPPERS WITH BEER CHEESE DIP

They may be funny looking, but these guys are serious business. These bites are hearty, salty, and smoky. Try serving these at your next super bowl party. The dip alone will keep everyone coming back for more.

Pan: 2 Mini 24-cup muffin pans

YOU WILL NEED:

Ingredients:
1 ½ cups warm (105–110°F) water
1 tbsp granulated sugar
1 packet active dry yeast
4 ½ cups all purpose flour
2 tsp kosher salt
4 tbsp unsalted butter, melted
10 cups or 3 quarts of water
⅔ cup baking soda
1 or 2 packages of cocktail sausage or mini
    hot dogs

1 egg yolk, beaten with 1 tbsp water
Kosher or Sea Salt

Cheese Dip
1 bottle of dark beer (I prefer Newcastle)
3 cups sharp cheddar, grated
2 tbsp flour
8 oz cream cheese or Neufchatel cheese,
    softened
2 cloves garlic, minced
Salt and pepper to taste

Directions:

1. Preheat oven to 425°F and grease two mini muffin pans.

2. In the stand mixer bowl, combine the warm water, sugar, and kosher salt. Sprinkle yeast on top and allow to sit for 5 minutes or until it begins to foam. Add the flour next, followed by the melted butter.

3. In a stand mixer with the hook attachment, knead the dough on medium speed for 4–5 minutes. When the dough is smooth and begins to pull away from the sides, turn the mixer off and turn the dough out. Clean and then oil the same mixing bowl and return the dough. Cover in plastic wrap and let it sit in a warm place for about an hour. Check on the dough, and at about 45 minutes in, start your pot of boiling water. You can use a pasta pot or a roasting pan. The roasting pan will allow for more dough to be boiled at a time.

4. While the dough is rising, start on the beer cheese dip. In a sauce pan over medium heat, bring beer to a simmer. In a bowl toss the cheese and flour together and add the beer. Finally add the softened cream cheese and garlic. Stir until the cheese has melted. The texture should be smooth. The whole process should take about 5 minutes. You can strain the mixture, if you'd like, through a fine mesh strainer. Keep warm until ready to serve.

5. When the dough has doubled in size, remove the dough from the pan and split into 48 equal pieces. I use the half method. Cut the dough in half, then each half in half and so on until you reach 48 pieces.

6. Add the baking soda to the water. Take each piece of dough and flatten as wide as it will go. Place a cocktail wiener in the middle and wrap the dough around it. Work in batches of four or five at a time, depending on the size of the pan. Boil each dough and dog combo for 20–30 seconds. Remove with a slotted spoon and place directly into each mini muffin cup.

7. After you have made all 48 little pretzel dogs, brush all the dogs with the egg wash and salt the dogs liberally.

8. Bake for 15–18 minutes. They should be a deep golden brown. Give the dip a stir to eliminate any film and serve with the pretzel dogs.

Note: *When I made this recipe, I also made the Brie and Jam Pretzel Buns (pg 15) for breakfast. You can use half the batch of dough for these and half for the pretzel buns.*

MELON SALAD IN PROSCIUTTO NESTS

Prosciutto e Melone. Mmm! If you let me eat that every day of my life, I would. Add crusty French bread and creamy brie cheese to that, it would definitely be my "stranded on a desert island" meal. Putting this traditional Italian appetizer into a muffin pan was a no-brainer for me. This new spin on an old classic will surely make a prosciutto and melon fan out of anyone.

***Pan:* Standard 12-cup muffin pan**

YOU WILL NEED:

Ingredients:
12 pieces of prosciutto
1 whole cantaloupe, cubed or balled

2 tbsp pine nuts
2 tbsp chopped mint
1 tbsp olive oil
Balsamic vinegar

Directions:

1. Preheat the oven to 375°F.
2. In a large bowl, toss the cantaloupe, chopped mint, and olive oil together.
3. Place one end of the prosciutto slice on the bottom of the muffin cup. Wrap the prosciutto around the inside of the muffin cup until it meets back at the start of the wrap. Give it a stretch until it reaches. This technique can take a few tries. You can use foil balls (a sheet of foil crumpled up into a ball shape) to hold the prosciutto in place.
4. Bake for 10 minutes for a softer cups or as long as 15 minutes for a crispy shell.
5. Once baked, remove from the oven and allow to cool. When the prosciutto is ready place a spoonful of the cantaloupe mint salad in the cup. I found I could fit 3 mini cantaloupe balls.
6. Add a few pine nuts and drizzle the prosciutto and melon cups with balsamic vinegar.

Mix It Up: *Prosciutto cups can be filled with other yummy ingredients such as goat cheese and figs or tomatoes and mozzarella.*

ROASTED TOMATO TARTS WITH WHIPPED FETA AND HERB OIL

When serving this appetizer, I always use the whole description. "Whipped feta and herb oil" just sounds so fancy and complicated. In actuality, they are some of the easiest things in this book to make. And that's just how I like my food: fancy sounding but easy to make.

Pan: Mini 24-cup muffin pan

YOU WILL NEED:

Ingredients:
1 sheet puff pastry
24 cherry tomatoes
fresh thyme

Whipped Feta
1 ½ cups crumbled feta
½ cup whipping cream

Herb Oil
1 cup fresh basil
2 tbsp pine nuts
½ cup fresh parsley
1 clove garlic
½ tsp lemon zest
1 tsp lemon juice
½ cup extra virgin olive oil
Salt and pepper to taste

Directions:

1. Preheat the oven to 400°F. Grease the wells of a 24-cup mini pan.

2. Place 24 tomatoes in a large bowl. Using the bottom of a glass or back of a wooden spoon, squish the tomatoes to remove the seeds and pulp. Rinse the tomatoes and set aside.

3. Using a pizza cutter or very sharp knife, cut the puff pastry into 6 strips and then cut across 4 times, creating 24 squares. Place a square into each cup. Par bake for 7 minutes.

4. While in the oven, throw together the whipped feta. In a food processor or compact blender with whipping attachment, add the whipping cream and feta. Whip for a minute or until stiff peaks.

5. After 7 minutes, take the puff pastry out of the oven. Place a small dollop (very technical term) of the whipped feta in each cup. Place a cherry tomato on top.

6. For an extra boost of flavor, add a pinch of the chopped thyme to the top before backing.

7. Put the tarts back in the oven for another 5–6 minutes. Check to see if the cheese is bubbling and the puff pastry is golden brown.

8. While that is in the oven, mix up the herb oil. Add all of the herb oil ingredients in a blender or a food processor and pulse until it has the consistency of a thin pesto sauce. Serve herb oil alongside the tomato tarts.

Note: *I really do think this recipe is pretty impressive. The herb oil and whipped feta make for a great appetizer in itself. If you have leftovers, toast up some French bread or sourdough and serve with dinner. Or eat an entire loaf of bread with spread and oil in one sitting . . . Wait, what? No, I didn't do that.*

SALAMI BOATS WITH ANTIPASTO SALAD

Almost every family get-together at my parent's house includes a platter of assorted Italian meats and cheeses from our neighborhood delicatessen, Lucca's. This deli is great becuse it is so close to the house and has the best Italy has to offer. We almost always order salami, prosciutto, cappicola, fontina, and parmesan. (Oh, I am making myself hungry.) Very rarely are there leftovers. The last party we had, I made sure to save some of the salami from the platter to try out on this dish.

Pans: **Standard 12-cup muffin pan**

YOU WILL NEED:

Ingredients:
12 slices of genoa salami
1 cup cherry
    tomatoes, halved
1 cup pearl mozzarella balls
½ cup of the following:
    marinated artichokes
    marinated mushrooms

¼ cup of the following:
    green olives
    chopped pepperoncini
1 tbsp Italian seasoning
1 tbsp grated garlic
Shaved/grated Italian hard cheeses
    (pecorino romano, parmesan,
    asiago, etc.) as a garnish

Directions:

1. Preheat the oven to 400°F. While the oven is heating up, mix all the ingredients, excluding the grated Italian cheeses, in a large bowl.
2. Place a piece of salami into the well of each muffin cup. To keep the salami in its bowl shape, crumple up a piece of foil into a ball shape and place inside salami cup while it bakes.
3. Bake for 10–12 minutes or until the salami is crisp.
4. Let the salami cool before filling the cup with antipasto. Top with the grated cheese.

Note: *If you have some of the antipasto mixture left over, I recommend throwing it into some pasta. Hot or cold it's definitely a winner!*

SMOKED GOUDA AND SOYRIZO JALAPEÑO POPPERS

The standard jalapeño poppers get kicked up with the edition of the soyrizo and smoked gouda.

Pan: **Mini 24-cup muffin pan**

YOU WILL NEED:

Ingredients:
10 oz Soyrizo
1 can of crescent rolls
1 cup smoked gouda, shredded
¼ cup red onions, finely chopped
1 egg

4 oz cream cheese
3 tbsp sour cream
1 tbsp hot sauce
1–2 large jalapeno peppers,
    stemmed, seeded, and halved
Salt and pepper, to taste

Directions:

1. Preheat the oven to 350°F and grease a mini muffin pan.

2. Brown soyrizo over medium heat. After 3 or 4 minutes, drain the soyrizo and place in a large mixing bowl. Add the gouda, onion, egg, cream cheese, sour cream, and hot sauce to the bowl. Mix all the ingredients together. Add salt and pepper to taste.

3. Prepare the crescent dough by splitting each crescent triangle in half, creating two triangles. Place a tsp of the mixture into the center of the dough. Fold the three points into the center. Press the seams together to create a seal. Place the dough, seam side down into the muffin pan.

4. Bake at 350°F for 10–12 minutes.

Note: *If you have a hard time finding blocks of smoked gouda in the store, try heading over to the deli counter. Ask for ½ lb of the cheese, unsliced. If your local deli is like mine and without smoked gouda, and you don't feel like driving all over the place for cheese, smoked gouda slices, very finely chopped, will work as well.*

MINI SPANIKOPITA

These little spinach feta pies work well in both a standard pan and a mini muffin pan. They are very quick to put together and very tasty.

Pan: **Standard 12-cup muffin pan**

YOU WILL NEED:

Ingredients:

1 (10 oz) package frozen chopped spinach
1 small onion, finely chopped
3 green onions, whites only
Handful parsley, chopped
¼ tsp nutmeg

4 oz feta, crumbled
½ cup ricotta or cottage cheese
1 egg, beaten
¼ cup pine nuts
Salt and pepper, to taste
1 box phyllo, thawed
4 tbsp butter, melted

Directions:

1. Preheat oven at 375°F and grease muffin pan with butter.

2. In a skillet, heat olive oil over medium heat. Add both chopped onions and cook until tender, 3–4 minutes.

3. In a large bowl, microwave spinach for 1–2 minutes. Line a strainer with several paper towels and pour in spinach. Gather the edges of the paper towel and squeeze the bundle of spinach over the strainer. For cooking in pastry it is important to have very dry spinach. Continue to squeeze the spinach until all the water has been drained out.

4. Add the spinach back to the large bowl and add feta, ricotta, egg, and pine nuts. Add onions to the bowl and season with salt and pepper to taste.

5. Remove phyllo from the refrigerator and place on a cutting board. Using a sharp knife or pizza cutter, cut 8–9 sheets of phyllo into 4x4 inch squares.

6. Start by placing 2 squares of phyllo on the bottom of each muffin cup. Press into the bottom of the cup and dab or brush butter on the phyllo squares. Continue with another layer of 1–2 phyllo squares, pressing down to create a cup, add more butter, and then a final layer of 1–2 sheets of phyllo and a touch more melted butter.

7. To each phyllo cup, add a heaping tablespoon of spinach filling. Fold edges of the phyllo down on top of the filling.

8. Bake for 15 minutes, or until the edges are golden brown.

CREAMY SOUTHWEST BEGGAR'S PURSE

These beggar's purses are great for entertaining. I like to make large batches and freeze some for future parties.

Pan: **Mini 12-cup muffin pan**

YOU WILL NEED:

Ingredients:
1 sheets of puff pastry
½ avocado, cubed
¼ cup cream cheese
¼ cup chipotle salsa

2 green onions, whites
    chopped, greens reserved
Handful cilantro, chopped
1 egg, beaten
Salt and pepper, to taste

Directions:

1. Preheat oven to 400°F and grease a 12-cup mini muffin pan.

2. Divide a sheet of puff pastry into 12 small squares. Fill each puff pastry square before placing in the muffin pan. Place one cube of avocado and ½ tsp each of cream cheese and salsa. Top with several pieces of green onion.

3. Bring the four corners of the puff pastry to the top around the toppings, pressing the sides together, and place in a muffin cup. Using the green part of a green onion, wrap the top, where the puff pastry corners meet, like a gift bag.

4. Bake for 20 minutes.

CAPRESE
POLENTA BITES

This recipe is perfect for a small dinner party. Prepare the polenta in advance so that when the guests arrive you can finish off this dish quickly. I like serving it as a side dish with rosemary roasted chicken and grilled asparagus but they also make a great appetizer. Red wine optional but highly recommended.

***Pan:* Mini 24-cup muffin pan**

YOU WILL NEED:

Ingredients:

12 oz (½ lb tube) of precooked
    Polenta, cubed
12 mozzarella pearls
12 cherry tomatoes

2 ½ tbsp olive oil
1 tbsp balsamic vinegar
3 cloves garlic, minced
Salt and pepper, to taste
3–4 leaves of basil, chiffonade

Directions:

1. Preheat oven to 350°F and grease a mini muffin pan and line a baking sheet with a silpat or parchment paper.
2. Cut tomatoes in half lengthwise, and place in a medium sized mixing bowl. Toss with olive oil, balsamic, and garlic. Spread tomatoes out on prepared baking sheet, sprinkle with salt and pepper, and bake for 35–40 minutes, or until soft and slightly blistered.
3. Place cubed polenta in a microwave safe dish. Heat for 2 minutes and stir with a fork until mushy.
4. Fill the cups halfway with the soft polenta. Add a mozzarella pearl.
5. Bake the polenta for 13–15 minutes, or until the cheese is melted.
6. Serve warm polenta cup topped with a roasted tomato and a slice of fresh basil, using a toothpick to hold it all in place.

APRICOT BRIE TARTS WITH CHIPOTLE HONEY ALMONDS

While brainstorming one afternoon, my friend Kelly and I tried to come up with a recipe to use some leftover brie from a dinner party. This recipe was the brainchild of that conversation. She suggested, in a very convincing way, that apricots and brie make a killer combination and I have to agree. We threw around some other ingredients to add to it and landed on chipotle almonds. The spice really makes the dish stand out. The result is sweet chewy apricots, salty creamy brie, and spicy crunchy chipotle almonds. It really is killer.

Pan: Mini 24-cup muffin pan

YOU WILL NEED:

Ingredients:

1 roll of puff pastry, thawed in fridge
150 g of brie cheese, about a 2-in
    slice, cubed into 24 pieces
12 dried apricots, sliced half
    lengthwise
1 cup sliced almonds

2 tbsp unsalted butter
2 tbsp honey
1 tsp chipotle pepper powder
1 tsp sugar
½ tsp salt
¼ tsp garlic powder
¼ tsp cinnamon

Directions:

1. Preheat oven to 350°F and line a baking tray with your silpat or parchment paper.
2. Melt the butter in a pan over medium heat until it starts to give off a yummy nutty smell. It should only take a few minutes to brown the butter. Careful not to let the butter burn. When you feel it is done, take the pan off the heat. Add the almonds to the pan and coat with the browned butter.
3. Turn the almonds out on the baking tray and bake for 10 minutes. Meanwhile prepare your spice mixture. In a bowl large enough to hold all the almonds, add the chipotle powder, sugar, salt, garlic powder, and cinnamon. Give it a quick mix with a fork to ensure the mixture is well combined. Take the tray from the oven and give the almonds a stir to ensure no sides are getting too brown.
4. Put the tray back in the oven for another 5 minutes.
5. After 5 minutes, take the almonds from the oven and pour into the bowl with the spices. Give the almonds a quick toss in the mixture until completely coated.
6. Turn the oven up to 400°F and grease a 24-cup mini muffin pan.
7. Allow the almonds to cool for a little while the puff pastry is prepared. Using a sharp knife or pizza cutter, cut the puff pastry into 24 squares.
8. Place one square of puff pastry into the well of each cup.
9. Into each puff pastry square add one cube of brie, 1 tsp of chipotle almonds and finally top it with a halved apricot.
10. Cook at 400°F for 11–13 minutes. Keep an eye on the dish so it doesn't get too brown. With the sugar in the apricot and almonds this dish has a tendency to burn. Start with 11 minutes and add more time if needed.

CHICKEN PARMESAN CRACKER CUPS

These cracker cups always come with the same question "How did you get the cracker into the muffin cups?" And I always answer the same way, "Magic!" Well okay, it's not magic but these cracker cups are easy to pull off with just a little know-how.

***Pan:* Mini 24-cup muffin pan**

YOU WILL NEED:

Ingredients:
24 roasted garlic woven wheat
    crackers
2 eggs
½ cup water

24 mozzarella pearls
1 cup chicken, cooked
    and diced
¼ cup pasta sauce
Italian seasonings

Directions:

1. Preheat oven to 350°F and spray a mini muffin pan.
2. In a pie plate beat together eggs and water until well combined. Place 12 crackers, or as many as will fit in the pie pan. Let the crackers stand for 4 minutes, turning once at 2 minutes. Repeat with the final 12 crackers.
3. Carefully place one cracker into the well of a mini muffin cup.
4. Bake crackers for 30 minutes.
5. Remove pan from the oven. Carefully add a cube of chicken, ½ tsp of sauce on top of the chicken. Finally top with mozzarella and a sprinkle of seasonings.
6. Bake for an additional 5–6 minutes, until cheese is bubbly and brown.

BLAT CHICKEN SALAD IN WONTON CUPS

I am not a picky eater. There is very little I refuse to eat and I will always try food offered to me. The one exception, however, is mayonnaise. I really, really don't like mayo. So naturally, I was never a big fan of chicken or tuna salad. Then I discovered the beauty of avocado chicken salad. It has the creaminess of a traditional chicken salad but without all the mayo. Hurray for avocados!

Pan: **Standard 12-cup muffin pan**

YOU WILL NEED:

Ingredients:

Wonton wrappers
2 cups chicken, shredded
2 avocados, cubed
2 tbsp cilantro, chopped
2 green onions, chopped
1 lime, juiced

1 tomato, diced
4 strips of bacon, cooked
  and chopped
Salt & pepper, to taste
1 cup of lettuce or cabbage,
  shredded and chopped

Directions:

1. Preheat oven to 375°F and spray a standard muffin pan.
2. Place 2–3 wrappers in the wells of the muffin pan, overlapping them to fit to create a cup.
3. Spray the wonton cup with cooking spray to protect them from burning.
4. Bake for 10–13 minutes, until the edges begin to brown and the cups are crispy.
5. While the wonton cups bake, prepare the chicken salad.
6. In a large bowl, add the avocado cubes and mash with a fork. Add in the cilantro, green onions, and lime juice and mix together.
7. Add in the chicken, tomatoes, and bacon and give the whole mixture a good stir.
8. Place a generous amount of lettuce into each cup.
9. Divide the chicken salad amongst the cups and serve immediately.

Note: *To serve this recipe as an appetizer, place 1 wonton wrapper in the cup of the mini muffin pan. The chicken salad can be made the night before. Bake the cups the day you plan to serve them.*

ITTY BITTY LOBSTA ROLLS

Every summer, my big Italian family gets together on the Cape for a family reunion. We swim, catch up, go to the movies, share stories, and soak in family time. It's just plain wonderful. One of my favorite parts about being back east, besides hanging out with all my crazy cousins, is the food. My Uncle Carl makes quahogs casinos, we buy cold cuts and make monster sandwiches, go out for pizza, get ice cream, and the ultimate treat . . . lobster rolls. I look forward to these every year. I made these mini lobster rolls in honor of my fun family. I love you guys. I'll see you all next year!

Pan: **Standard 12-cup muffin pan**

YOU WILL NEED:

Ingredients:
6 slices sourdough or white bread
Butter
½ lb cooked lobster meat, chopped
1 stalk celery, diced

2 tbsp mayonnaise or greek yogurt
¼ tsp Old Bay seasoning
2 tbsp lemon juice
2 tbsp chives, chopped
1 tsp sea salt

Directions:

1. Preheat oven 350°F and spray 6 wells of a standard muffin pan.
2. Butter both sides of the bread. Cut the bread into a square by cutting off the crusts. Place the bread in the muffin cups.
3. Bake for 8–10 minutes, or until golden brown
4. In a bowl, combine lobster, mayonnaise, Old Bay, lemon juice, chives and salt.
5. When the bread bowls are finished, allow them to cool completely. Fill the bread bowls with lobster mixture. Garnish with chives.

MINI CORN AND CRAB CAKES

My sister and I have this weird thing about crab cakes and corn. As a San Franciscan, I love crab and crab cakes. My sister Becky does not. She loves corn from a can. I do not. Seemingly unrelated but it's one of those weird sister inside jokes from when we were kids. You had to pick a side: Corn or Crab Cakes. We've had a weird battle ever since. It's definitely silly sister stuff but if you have a sister, you probably have your own weird things. Well, the irony is that you don't really need to choose one or the other when it comes to corn and crab. They actually compliment each other very well, just like my sister and I do. So here is my version of a mini crab AND corn cake; the best of both worlds for my little sister. "You and me baby, we're stuck like glue." Love you, Sis.

Pan: Standard 24-cup mini muffin pan

YOU WILL NEED:

Ingredients:

8 oz cream cheese, room temperature
1 cup parmesan cheese
1 large egg
¼ cup sour cream
1 tsp orange zest
1 tsp lemon zest

3 tbsp chives, plus more for garnish
¼ kosher salt
¼ tsp cayenne pepper
8 oz lump crab meat, patted dry
¼ cup corn kernels, charred
½ cup panko bread crumbs
2 tbsp unsalted butter, melted

Directions:

1. Preheat oven to 350°F and generously butter a mini muffin pan.

2. In a food processor or using a hand-held mixer and medium sized bowl, beat the cream cheese until smooth. Add ¼ cup of parmesan and egg and blend. Mix in sour cream, zests, 1 tablespoon chives, salt, and cayenne. Using a fork, coarsely shred the crab meat. Fold in the shredded crab meat and the corn kernels.

3. Cover the bowl and chill while you prepare the bread crumbs.

4. In a small bowl, toss the remaining ½ cup of parmesan, panko, and the remaining 2 tablespoons of chives together. Drizzle melted butter over the panko mixture and toss with a fork until evenly coated and moistened. Press one tablespoon of the panko mixture into the muffin cup, creating a crust. Scoop a little more than a tablespoon of the crab and corn mixture into the panko crust. Top the crabmeat with a tsp of the panko mixture.

5. Bake for 30 minutes or until the panko topping is golden brown. Allow the Mini crab cakes to cool in the pan for 5 minutes before de-panning. Run a knife around the edge of the muffin cup to help lift the crab cake from the pan.

CARAMELIZED ONION & BALSAMIC FIG HAND PIES

Carmelized onions, figs and goat cheese? It really doesn't get much better than that.

Pan: **1 Standard 12-cup muffin pan**

YOU WILL NEED:

Ingredients:

12 sheets of phyllo, thawed
1 tsp sugar
1 large yellow onion, thinly sliced
1 tbsp butter, plus more for the muffin
    pan
$\frac{1}{8}$ tsp baking soda
1 tsp salt
Pepper, to taste

2 cups figs, coarsely chopped
$\frac{1}{8}$ cup balsamic vinegar
2 tbsp sugar
$\frac{1}{8}$ cup honey
2 tsp thyme leaves
$\frac{1}{8}$ tsp salt
2 tbsp cornstarch
4 tbsp butter
$\frac{1}{2}$ cup goat cheese

Directions:

1. Preheat the oven to 400°F and butter a standard muffin pan.

2. In a skillet, over medium-high heat, heat sugar until melted and light brown, about 3 minutes. Add onions and stir with a wooden spoon until coated with sugar. Add butter, baking soda, salt and pepper. Stir onions and continue to cook until all the liquid is cooked out. There should be a brown coating on the bottom of the pan after 6–8 minutes.

3. To deglaze the pan, add 1 tablespoon of water and scrape brown bits off the bottom of the pan. Stir occasionally until coating begins to appear again, an additional 3 minutes. Add one more tablespoon of water and scrape the pan down again. Repeat this process, cook for 3 minutes or so until coating forms, add water, scrape down until all the water is used and onions are a rich deep brown color. Remove from the pan and allow to rest in a bowl at room temperature.

4. In a large bowl, mix together figs with the balsamic, sugar, honey, thyme, and salt in a medium bowl. Allow the figs to macerate in the balsamic mixture for about 15 minutes. The mixture can sit overnight if preparing this dish the night before.

5. In the meantime, prepare the phyllo cups.

6. Put one pastry sheet on a cutting board. Brush with a little melted butter and top with a second sheet. Brush again with butter and top with the third sheet. Fold pastry in half, short end to short end. Lay the phyllo over the openings of 6 muffin cups. Brush with a little more butter and gently press into the muffin cups. Repeat the process with 3 more layers of buttered phyllo, folded and placed over the remaining 6 cups. Place in the fridge.

7. When you are ready to prepare the hand pies, carefully pour out 2 tablespoons of the liquid from the figs and mix in the cornstarch to thicken the filling. Add caramelized onions to the bowl and mix together.

8. Spoon a heaping tablespoon of the mixture into the phyllo cups. Add a dollop, about 2 tsps, of goat cheese on top of the fig and onion mixture.

9. Create 2 more phyllo stacks, layered, buttered, and folded the same as the bottom layer.

10. Brush more butter around the edges of the phyllo cup openings. Lay the second two stacks of phyllo on top and press to seal. Brush the remaining butter over the top and season with salt. Trim any phyllo hanging over the edge of the muffin pan.

11. Bake for 10–15 minutes, or until golden brown and crisp. Turn the pastry out onto a cutting board and using a sharp knife or pizza cutter, cut the pastry into 12 hand pies.

Side Dishes

BACON JALAPEÑO CHEDDAR CORNBREAD MUFFINS

As a kid, my brother Joey wanted to be a firefighter. At six years old, it isn't that unique. As a teacher I hear kids say they want to be a firefighter or police officer, basketball player, "animal doctor," or a fairy princess ninja warrior, of course. While kids grow up, go to school, and change their mind a hundred times, my brother held on to that dream of being a firefighter. When he was accepted into the SFFD Fire Reserve I was a very proud big sister. That is why I dedicate this recipe to him. When I think of firefighters, I think of firefighters in the kitchen cooking chili for each other in their down time. Doesn't everyone? And when I think of a good pot of chili, it is hard not to think of cornbread. My brother is a good cook in his own right so I imagine any station he lands in he'll impress even the veterans with his own dishes. But I hope, as a proud younger brother, he'll show off a few of his big sister's recipes too.

Love you, Joe.

Pan: Standard 12-cup muffin pan

YOU WILL NEED:

Ingredients:

2 (8.5 oz) boxes corn muffin mix

2 eggs

⅔ cup buttermilk

4 slices of bacon

½ cup cheddar cheese, shredded

½–1 jalapeño, seeded and diced

Directions:

1. Preheat the oven to 400°F and grease the muffin pan.
2. In a skillet, cook the bacon until crisp and set aside on a plate with a paper towel. Reserve the drippings.
3. In a large bowl, mix together egg and buttermilk. To that, stir in contents of corn muffin mix and 2 tablespoon of the reserved bacon drippings.
4. Chop the bacon into small pieces and fold into corn muffin mixture. Finally, fold in jalapeño and cheese into the mix and stir until combined. The amount of jalapeño depends on taste. To achieve crowns, or rounded tops, on the corn muffins, allow the batter to rest 3–4 minutes before baking.
5. Divide batter evenly among the 12 cups.
6. Bake for 15–18 minutes or until a toothpick inserted into the center of the muffin comes out clean.

A little know how: *No buttermilk? No problem. Buttermilk is easily made using items you probably already have on hand. Fill a ⅓ measuring cup almost to the top with milk, fill the rest of the space with lemon juice. Allow the mixture to sit while you cook the bacon. That'll give it enough time to set.*

AVOCADO AND BEAN SALSA IN TORTILLA CUPS

These bean and tortilla cups are crazy simple and delicious. And healthy too! They make a great addition to enchilada night or a side dish for fajitas.

Pan: Standard 12-cup or 2 jumbo 6-cup muffin pans

YOU WILL NEED:

Ingredients:

12 corn tortillas (store bought or homemade, see Huevos Rancheros recipe on p. 28)

1 can (15 oz) pinto beans, drained and rinsed

½–1 whole jalapeño, diced

1 avocado, diced into small ½ inch squares

½ a lime, juiced

1 cup of cherry tomatoes, halved

½ cup red onion, chopped

¼ cup cilantro, chopped

3–4 tbsp champagne, rice wine, or white balsamic vinegar

1–2 tbsp olive oil

Salt and pepper, to taste

Fresh cheese, like cotija, crumbled

Directions:

1. Preheat the oven to 350 °F and lightly spray down your choice of pan.

2. In a large bowl, mix the beans, onion, jalapeño, cilantro, lime juice, tomatoes, and avocado. Drizzle in the vinegar and oil and toss together. Add salt and pepper to taste. Cover with plastic wrap and place in the refrigerator while tortillas bake.

3. In two batches of 6, cover the tortillas in a damp paper towel and heat in the microwave for 30 seconds. This makes them more pliable.

4. When the oven is ready, place each tortilla in the well of the muffin pan. You will have to fold one of the sides in to make it fit.

5. Bake for 20–25 minutes until they are crispy.

6. Allow for the cups to cool. Add a spoonful or two of bean salsa into each tortilla cup.

Mix It Up: *Both the standard and the jumbo muffin pans work well for this recipe. I suggest both because they offer very different shapes. The smaller pan is perfect for holding in the hand while the larger pan allows for a flat bottom, which is better for serving on a plate. I like this recipe because it really is up to you how you make the salsa. Like bell peppers? Add them. Want some cheese, maybe some cotija? Add it. No vinegar around? Leave it out. It'll taste great however you make it.*

BROWN BUTTER SAGE SWEET POTATO PUFFS WITH GOAT CHEESE AND ROASTED GRAPES

I adore sweet potatoes. Add goat cheese to them and some brown buttered sage and I am in heaven! You might be too after you try these.

Pan: **Standard 12-cup muffin pan**

YOU WILL NEED:

Ingredients:

2 eggs

⅓ cup goat cheese

2 tbsp parmesan, grated

3 cups of mashed sweet potatoes

1 tbsp fresh thyme, chopped

2 tbsp butter

2 tbsp sage, finely sliced

2 cups red grapes

1 tbsp olive oil

Salt & pepper, to taste

Honey

Directions:

1. Preheat the oven to 400°F and grease muffin pan.
2. In a large mixing bowl, whisk together eggs and sour cream. Mix in cheeses and thyme.
3. If using leftover sweet potatoes, taste to see if they need any salt or pepper. When satisfied, add potatoes to bowl and mix well.
4. In a separate bowl, coat grapes in olive oil and sprinkle with salt and pepper. Spread grapes out on a greased baking sheet.
5. Divide the potatoes into the muffin cups and put both the baking sheet and muffin pan into the oven.
6. Bake for 30 minutes or until the potatoes begin to pull away from the sides of the cup and turn golden brown, this is also when the grapes begin to burst.
7. Remove both pans from the oven. Allow the grapes to cool slightly.
8. Serve sweet potatoes topped with roasted grapes and drizzled with honey.

BROWN SUGAR BAKED BEANS IN BACON BOWLS

I am a huge fan of bacon. I have several recipes in this cookbook featuring bacon. So, creating a serving dish made entirely of bacon seemed like the next logical step in my obsession. Baked beans made with more bacon also seemed like a perfectly normal amount of bacon to me. I imagine these bean bowls being served up at a backyard BBQ, complete with ribs, corn on the cob, and lots and lots of napkins.

Pan: **Standard 6-cup muffin pan**

YOU WILL NEED:

Ingredients:

1 cans (29 oz can) can of baked beans
3 slices thick-cut bacon
½ onion, chopped

¼ cup barbecue sauce
3 tbsp brown sugar
1 tbsp cider vinegar
½ tsp dry mustard
9 slices of bacon, for bowls

Directions:

1. Preheat oven to 325°F and grease a small baking dish.

2. In a large skillet, preferably cast iron, fry bacon until partially cooked. Remove bacon to a plate to drain. Reserve the drippings. To the same pan add the onions and cook until tender. Once the onions are cooked, add the beans, bbq sauce, brown sugar, vinegar, and dry mustard to the pan. Mix ingredients together and bring the whole pan to a simmer.

3. Turn the heat off and move the beans to the baking dish. Mix bacon into the beans, and bake at 325°F oven for 50 minutes.

4. When the beans are cooked, raise the oven heat to 400°F and grease a 6-cup standard muffin pan.

5. Each muffin cup gets 3 halves or 1 ½ pieces of bacon in total. Cut all the slices of bacon in half. Place two halves of bacon on the bottom of each cup in an X shape. Stretch the bacon up the sides. Take the remaining half and stretch it around the inside of the muffin cup. Press pieces of bacon together as firmly as possible. The fat in the bacon will help the piece stick together. You can also use a fork to press the fat together.

6. To ensure it holds its cup shape, loosely ball up a piece of foil and place in the center of the bacon cups. This will help ensure the bacon doesn't curl up.

7. Bake bacon bowls for 20–25 minutes, or until the bowls are crisp. Bacon will continue to cook outside of the oven. Some people like crispier bacon than others. Cook it to your preference. Then add the beans and enjoy.

MINI BRUSSELS SPROUT GRATIN

Please don't let the laundry list of ingredients scare you off from trying this dish. The added touches of lemon zest, parsley, and bacon give the Brussels sprouts a huge flavor boost. Try serving it at your next dinner party. It is sure to be a big hit.

***Pan:* Standard 12-cup muffin pan**

YOU WILL NEED:

Ingredients:

1 lb. Brussels sprouts, rinsed, peeled and quartered

5–6 cloves garlic, whole and unpeeled

3 tbsp olive oil

6 shallots, peeled and thinly sliced

3 slices bacon, chopped

1 tbsp lemon juice

1 tbsp unsalted butter

2 tsp flour

1 cup heavy cream

2 sprigs thyme, whole

1 tbsp water

2 tsp cornstarch

1 cup parmesan cheese, grated

½ cup panko bread crumbs

2 tsp parsley, finely chopped

2 tsp lemon zest

3 tbsp gruyere cheese, grated

1 tsp salt

¼ tsp pepper

2 tsp unsalted butter, melted

Directions:

1. Preheat oven 400°F and spray a standard muffin pan and baking sheet.

2. On a piece of foil, place cloves of garlic and drizzle with 2 tablespoons of olive oil. Fold foil over and create a pouch around the garlic. Seal up the edges and roast in the oven for 15 minutes. Remove from oven and allow to cool. Remove garlic from foil and press clove from the peel. Set garlic aside.

3. In a large mixing bowl, toss sprouts with a tablespoon of olive oil, salt, and pepper. Spread sprouts out in a single layer on greased baking sheet. Roast at 400°F for 10 minutes, or until sprouts are browned. Transfer Brussels sprouts into a large bowl.

4. In a large pan over medium high heat, sauté shallots and bacon, stirring frequently. Sauté until bacon is cooked and shallots begin to caramelize, about 4 minutes. Add 1 tablespoon of lemon zest and the cloves of roasted garlic. Deglaze the pan with lemon juice. Stir and remove pan from heat. Pour contents of the pan into the bowl with the Brussels sprouts. Stir the contents together. Set aside.

5. In a large saucepan over medium high heat, melt 1 tablespoon butter and add flour to make a roux. Cook for 30 seconds, until it's light brown. Add cream and thyme leaves, stirring to avoid lumps. Continue to stir for 2 minutes until it starts to simmer. In a small bowl stir together 1 tablespoon of water and 2 tsps of cornstarch to make a slurry. Mix well. Add the slurry to the cream and stir. The cream sauce should

start to thicken. Remove the pan from the heat and remove the sprigs of thyme. Return to the heat and add the parmesan cheese. Stir until cheese has melted. Season with salt and pepper to taste.

6. Carefully pour the cream sauce into the bowl with the Brussels sprouts and gently fold together.

7. Scoop the mixture into the cups of the muffin pan, filling them to the top. Press lightly to pack the Brussels sprouts into the bottom.

8. In a small bowl, mix together parsley, remaining 1 tablespoon lemon zest, gruyere, melted butter and salt and pepper to taste. Sprinkle the mixture on top of the Brussels sprouts. Spray a sheet of foil and cover the muffin pan, sprayed side down.

9. Bake covered for 15 minutes. Uncover and bake for an additional 5 minutes, or until top is browned. Allow the tray to rest for 10 minutes and serve from the muffin pan.

CRISPY CHEESY POTATO CUPS

If I had to choose a signature dish, I think this would be it. This is the dish that started my interest in cooking with the muffin pan. It was the first dish I made in the muffin pan for my family. I saw a similar dish being made on a cooking show and was instantly inspired. I looked up the recipe online and cooked it right away for dinner. As I improved my cooking skills I started to make the recipe my own. I included cornstarch to help bind the potatoes better, added bacon because I love it, and experimented with different cheeses. I am really happy with this final version.

Pan: Standard 12-cup muffin pan

YOU WILL NEED:

Ingredients:
½ cup panko bread crumbs
1 tbsp unsalted butter, softened
2 lbs russet potatoes, peeled and
    cubed
1 ¼ cup half and half
1 ¼ tsp salt

¾ tsp pepper
1 ⅓ cups swiss and gruyere cheese,
    shredded
⅔ cup Parmesan cheese, grated
2 tsp cornstarch
½ cup bacon, cooked
    and crumbled

Directions:

1. Preheat oven to 425°F, move oven rack to lowest position, and grease a standard muffin pan with butter.

2. Pulse panko crumbs in a food processor until finely ground and press ground panko into the sides of the cup.

3. In a large microwave safe bowl, combine potatoes, half & half, salt, and pepper. Cover the bowl with plastic wrap and microwave for 12–15 minutes, just until tender. Stir once.

4. While the potatoes are in the microwave, in a separate bowl, combine shredded cheese, parmesan, and cornstarch. Scoop ⅓ cup of the mixture and reserve for a topping.

5. When the potatoes are done, add the remaining cheese mixture to the bowl and stir until smooth. Evenly divide the potato mixture among the 12 cups. Top with the reserved cheese.

6. Spray the underside of a large piece of foil with cooking spray. Cover the potatoes, greased side down.

7. Bake for 10 minutes. Remove foil and bake for an additional 13–15 minutes, or until golden brown.

8. Run a knife around the potato cup. Allow to cool slightly in the muffin pan. Turn potatoes out on to a serving tray. Allow to cool for additional 5 minutes before serving.

LOADED MASHED POTATO PUFFS

If there was ever a perfect treat for a Super Bowl party, this recipe is it. Potatoes, bacon, cheese, and sour cream . . . a winning combination! Throw in some chives for good measure and you have yourself a recipe touchdown!

***Pan:* Standard 12-cup muffin pan, nonstick**

YOU WILL NEED:

Ingredients:

2 eggs
⅓ cup sour cream
1 cup sharp cheddar cheese, shredded
2 tbsp parmesan, grated

2 tbsp chives, chopped
3 strips of bacon, cooked and crumbled
3 cups mashed potatoes
Salt & pepper, to taste

Directions:

1. Preheat the oven to 400°F and grease muffin pan.
2. In a large mixing bowl, whisk together eggs and sour cream. Mix in cheeses and chives.
3. If using leftover mashed potatoes, taste the potatoes to see if they need any salt or pepper. When satisfied, add potatoes to bowl and mix well.
4. Divide the potatoes into the muffin cups.
5. Bake 30 minutes or until the potatoes begin to pull away from the sides of the cup and turn golden brown.
6. Let the puffs cool for several minutes in the pan.

MUFFIN PAN LATKES WITH CRANBERRY-APPLE COMPOTE

I built this recipe around the shredded hash browns. I love frozen hash browns and I wanted a dish that utilized them. I decided to make my own muffin pan latkes. I top them with this tart cranberry-apple compote, which I think really compliments the potatoes.

Pan: Standard 12-cup muffin pan

YOU WILL NEED:

Ingredients:
1 (20 oz) bag frozen shredded hash browns
1 onion, chopped
1 egg
1 tbsp all purpose flour
½ cup Parmesan cheese, grated
1 green onion, chopped
1 tbsp canola or olive oil
½ tsp salt
Pepper, to taste

Cranberry-Apple Compote
1 package (12 ounces) fresh or frozen cranberries
2 medium apples, peeled, cored, and diced into ½-inch chunks
¼ cup brown sugar
1 tbsp grated ginger (optional: use 1–2 tsps ground ginger instead)
Zest of one orange
¼ cup orange juice
1 tsp cinnamon
¼ tsp salt

Directions:

1. Preheat oven to 350°F and spray a 12-cup muffin pan.
2. In a large bowl, add the ingredients for the latkes and mix together. Divide potatoes among the 12 cups and press firmly into the cup.
3. Bake for 45–50 minutes.
4. While the potatoes are cooking, prepare the cranberry-apple compote. In a sauce pan, combine the ingredients for the compote and cook over medium heat until all the cranberries pop. Cook for additional 5–10 minutes. The sauce should be thick but still chunky. Remove from heat and cool.
5. At 45 minutes, check to see if the edges of potatoes are beginning to brown. The edges should be a deep golden brown but not burnt. Allow the potatoes to sit for 10 minutes before removing from pan.
6. Serve latkes with compote and sour cream.

FREEZER MINESTRONE SOUP

I make a lot of soups. Whenever I have leftover food like pasta, beans, sausage, spinach, etc., I throw it in a pot and call it soup. This recipe is for all the other soup lovers out there. This soup freezes really well and the muffin pan is a great way to portion out the just the right amount.

Pan: Silicone muffin pan, standard 12-cup or jumbo 6-cup

YOU WILL NEED:

Ingredients:

2 tbsp olive oil
1 small onion, minced
½ cup Italian green beans, cut and frozen
4 cups low sodium vegetable broth
1 (15 oz) can red kidney beans, drained
1 (15 oz) can cannellini beans, drained
1 (14 oz) can diced tomatoes
1 (8 oz) can tomato paste
½ cup carrot, shredded
2 cups hot water

2 tbsp fresh parsley, minced
1 ½ tsp dried oregano
½ tsp dried basil
¼ tsp dried thyme
½ tsp pepper
½ cup red wine
4 cloves garlic, minced
1 medium zucchini, thinly sliced
Salt, to taste
Small shell pasta, cooked al dente
Parmesan cheese, grated

Directions:

1. In a large soup pot, heat olive oil over medium high heat.
2. Saute onions and green beans in the soup pot for 5 minutes, or until onions are soft.
3. Add broth, beans, diced tomatoes with the liquid, tomato paste, carrots, hot water, parsley, oregano, basil, thyme, and pepper.
4. Bring the whole mixture to a boil. Reduce heat and simmer for 20 minutes.
5. Add zucchini and garlic and continue to cook for an additional 20 minutes, or until the soup reaches the desired consistency.
6. Remove the pot from the heat and allow it to reach room temperature, uncovered. Stir the pot occasionally to release more heat.
7. When the soup has reached room temperature, fill the silicone muffin cups and freeze, uncovered.
8. Once the soup is frozen, pop them out of the tray and place in a zip top bag to store. Press out as much as air as you can from the bag before returning to the freezer. Label the bag with the date. Frozen soup can last 6–8 weeks.
9. When you are ready to eat, take out the desired number of soup cups and reheat in the microwave. Half way through, add desired amount of pasta and continue to cook until the soup is nice and hot. Top with parmesan cheese.

Note: *There are several additions you can make to this soup. If you like your soup with celery, add ½ stalk sliced when sautéing the onions and green beans. Two cups spinach of fresh spinach can be used when the zucchini and garlic is added to the pot. You can omit the wine if you desire. This method works for freezing stock as well. I often use cheese tortellini instead of shell pasta when making this dish. It makes this dish less healthy but more hearty!*

SPICY QUINOA BITES

I have become such a fan of quinoa. I like to have it on hand for veggie bowls or salads like the Citrus Shrimp Taco Salad on p. 157. It makes a wonderful alternative to rice and is great kept in the freezer. When the mood strikes you, take some quinoa and mix up a batch of these spicy quinoa bites. Feel free to mix up the herbs and cheese. You could even add 1–2 cups of carrots, broccoli, or zucchini to this recipe if you wanted to make them really healthy.

Pan: **Mini 24-cup muffin pan**

YOU WILL NEED:

Ingredients:
2 cups cooked quinoa
¾ cups swiss, gruyere cheese or cheddar cheese, shredded
2 eggs, beaten
2 green onion, thinly sliced

1 clove garlic, minced
1 tbsp cilantro, chopped
1 tbsp honey
1 ½–2 tbsp sriracha
½ tsp salt
½ cup panko bread crumbs

Directions:

1. Preheat oven to 350°F and spray a mini muffin pan.
2. In a large bowl, stir together all the listed ingredients. The mixture should be thick and stick to the spoon. If the mixture seems too loose, add more breadcrumbs until it reaches the desired sticky consistency.
3. Using a mini cookie scoop or tablespoon, spoon the mixture into the 24 cups. Firmly press the quinoa down. Add more quinoa if there is space and press into the cup.
4. Bake for 15–20 minutes, or until the edges begin to brown. Rotate the pan halfway through.
5. Allow the quinoa bites to rest for 5 minutes in the pan before removing.

MINI CHEESY RANCH BROCCOLI RICE BAKE

These brown rice broccoli cups are a great way to get children to eat veggies. I know for me, as a kid, if you covered it in cheese, I'd eat almost anything. These are no exception.

***Pan:* Standard 12-cup muffin pan**

YOU WILL NEED:

Ingredients:
2 cups brown rice, cooked
2 cups broccoli, thawed and dry
    or fresh

2 cups shredded cheddar cheese
½ cup ranch dressing
4 eggs, beaten
Salt and pepper, to taste

Directions:

1. Preheat oven to 350°F and grease a standard muffin pan.
2. In a large bowl, mix together rice, broccoli, one cup of cheese, dressing, eggs, salt, and pepper until well combined.
3. Divide the rice among the 12 cups. Top with the remaining cup of cheese.
4. Bake for 25–30 minutes, or until edges begin to brown.
5. Run a knife around the edge to remove cleanly.

Note: *I usually use leftover rice for these and often switch up the cheese based on what I have on hand. Add leftover chicken or ham to this dish. Cook rice with broth for a richer flavor.*

GARLIC SHRIMP AND CHIVE MUFFINS

You read that correctly—this muffin has shrimp in it. Butter, garlic, and chives complement the shrimp in this muffin. Great for serving with a bisque or creamy soup.

Pan: Standard 12-cup muffin pan

YOU WILL NEED:

Ingredients:

12 medium shrimp, tails removed
4 cloves garlic, minced
2 tbsp butter
2 cups flour
¼ cup sugar
3 tsp baking powder
½ tsp salt
1 tsp pepper
1 tbsp lemon zest
2 tbsp chives, chopped
¾ cup milk
⅓ cup butter, melted
1 egg, beaten

Directions:

1. Preheat oven to 400°F and grease a muffin pan or line with baking cups.

2. In a cast iron skillet over medium heat, sauté butter and garlic for 30 seconds. Add shrimp and cook for 3–4 minutes. Remove from heat and add some salt to taste.

3. In a bowl, combine flour, baking powder, salt, pepper, lemon zest, and chives.

4. In a separate bowl whisk together milk, melted butter, and egg. Pour the wet ingredients into the dry and mix thoroughly.

5. Chop half the shrimp and add it to the batter. At this point the mixture is very thick, like a bread dough. I recommend using your hands to mix it. Split the other six shrimp down the middle.

6. Fill the cups with batter ¾ full. Place one half of shrimp on top of the batter.

7. Bake for 20–25 minutes or until golden brown. Insert a toothpick into the center until it comes out clean.

PARMESAN CHEESE CUPS WITH DIJON BRUSSELS SPROUT SALAD

I knew that if I wanted to add a salad to my list of recipes, I would have to get really creative. I had made parmesan cheese crisps before but when I discovered they could be pressed into the muffin cup, I knew exactly how to serve up this Brussels sprout salad.

***Pan:* Jumbo 6-cup muffin pan**

YOU WILL NEED:

Ingredients:
1 cup Brussels sprouts, shredded or thinly sliced
1 ½ cups parmesan
¼ cup almonds, sliced
¼ red onion, thinly sliced
Handful dried cranberries

Dressing:
1 lemon, juiced
1 tsp dijon
1 tsp olive oil
½ tsp honey
Salt and pepper, to taste

Directions:

1. Preheat oven to 325°F.
2. In a bowl, soak onion slices in cold water for 15 to 20 minutes while you prepare the other ingredients.
3. On a baking sheet, spread almond slices in a single layer. Drizzle the almonds with olive oil and a generous amount of coarse sea salt.
4. Toast almonds for 10–12 minutes or until light golden brown. Stir half way through.
5. On two separate baking sheets make six ¼ cup mounds of parmesan cheese on each tray, 12 in all. Gently pat the cheese to form thin circles. Sprinkle with pepper.
6. Bake for 8–10 minutes, or until the circle begin to brown. With the muffin pan ready, remove baking sheets from the oven using a spatula and quickly place cheese circles into the wells of the muffin pan. Gently press into the bottom of the muffin cup.
7. In a small bowl, whisk together lemon juice, mustard, salt, and pepper to taste. Whisk in olive oil until the dressing emulsifies.
8. Pour Brussels sprouts into a large bowl and separate Brussels sprouts with fingers until they resemble cold slaw.
9. Drain the onions and add them to bowl with the Brussels sprouts, along with toasted almonds and cranberries. Toss everything together with preferred amount of dressing.
10. Fill the parmesan cups with salad. Serve immediately.

CHEESY HERB POPOVERS

This recipe is great for using up whatever cheeses and herbs you may have in the fridge. I like the gruyere and chive combination or parmesan and basil. See the list in the note section for other tasty options.

Pan: Standard 12-cup muffin pan

YOU WILL NEED:

Ingredients:

1 cup whole or 2% milk
2 eggs
3 tbsp unsalted butter, melted

1 cup flour
¼ tsp salt
1 ¼ cup cheese, grated
2 tbsp herbs

Directions:

1. Preheat oven to 450°F and grease a standard muffin pan.

2. In a blender, mix milk, eggs, and 1 tablespoon of butter until completely combined. Add flour, salt, cheese, and herbs and blend until frothy. Let the mixture sit while the oven heats up. This allows the flour to absorb, which helps create a better texture.

3. Place the muffin pan in the oven for 2 minutes to heat the pan.

4. Remove the pan and divide the remaining butter among the 12 cups. Give the batter a final blend and pour the batter into the cups, filling them halfway.

5. Bake at 450°F for 15 minutes. Do not open the door while the popovers bake.

6. Reduce the oven temperature to 350°F and bake for an additional 15 minutes.

7. After 30 minutes have passed, it is safe to open the oven door and check on the popovers. They should be golden brown and dry.

8. Turn the popovers out onto a cooling rack. Pierce the bottom to allow the steam to escape. Allow the popovers to cool only until they can be handled safely, but are still warm.

Here is a list of suggestions for combining cheese and herbs.

Cheese: Gruyere • Parmesan • Cheddar • Swiss • Manchego • Blue Cheese (¼ cup)

Herbs: Chives • Rosemary • Basil • Parsley • Basil • Thyme

MINI PASTALONE

After grad school, I worked in Costa Rica for 6 months teaching English part time and exploring the country. During my time there I discovered a love for plantains. Any way you make them, sweet, savory, or fried I would devour them. When I returned home I found that fresh plantains were not always easy to come by. Then one day, I discovered plantains in the frozen section. They are already cooked and perfect for this dish.

Pan: Standard 12-cup muffin pan

YOU WILL NEED:

Ingredients:

2 (11 oz) packages of frozen sweet plantains

3 tbsp achiote or annatto oil

1 cup tomato sauce or sofrito, if it is available

¼ cup marinated olive, pimentos and caper combo, or alcaparrado finely chopped

½ tsp cumin

¼ tsp cinnamon

1 lb ground pork

1 tbsp tomato paste

½ cup raisins

1 tbsp unsalted butter

4 large eggs, beaten

Salt and pepper, to taste

Directions:

1. Preheat oven to 350°F and grease a standard muffin pan with butter.

2. In a medium size skillet, heat achiote oil and tomato sauce over medium high heat. Stir occasionally as the water begins to evaporate. Add olive, pimento and caper mix, cumin and cinnamon and pork to the skillet. Break up the large chunks of meat and stir to coat in the oil and spices with a wooden spoon. Mix in tomato paste and raisins and season with salt and pepper to taste. Stir all the ingredients together well and remove from heat when the meat is cooked through.

3. Prepare the plantains by slicing each one in half lengthwise. This will help heat the plantains evenly. Begin to layer your muffin cups by placing smaller pieces of plantain on the bottom. You may need to cut pieces in half again to ensure the bottom is covered. Place two or three more slices of plantains around the edge. Spoon the meat mixture on top of the plantains, filling the cups almost to the top.

4. Evenly and slowly divide the eggs among the cups, allowing the egg mixture to move into the empty spaces in the cup.

5. Bake at 350°F for 20 minutes or until the dish is golden brown. Run a knife around the edge to loosen the cups. Gently, using a spoon or fork, lift the pastelon out of the muffin pan. Serve hot.

Note: *If you have the option, use sofrito in place of tomato sauce. Sofrito is a sauce most commonly used in Puerto Rican food. It is a combination of bell peppers, tomatoes, onion, garlic, cilantro and parsley. If sofrito isn't sold where you live, look for a tomato sauce with peppers, onions, and garlic and add your own fresh cilantro and parsley. If you are also having a problem finding achiote oil, olive oil and turmeric can be used as a substitute in a pinch.*

SAUSAGE AND MUSHROOM STUFFIN' MUFFINS

I am usually in charge of potatoes for our big Thanksgiving feast and I usually make the crispy potato cups on p. 123 or the sweet potato puffs on p. 115. But as the unofficial "Muffin Lady," I feel like I need to step out of the box for Thanksgiving. I have seen stuffin' muffins all over the internet but I like this version the best. It uses my two favorite stuffing ingredients: sausage and mushrooms. I hope you try these at your next Thanksgiving meal. But be careful, you might be in charge of stuffing from then on.

Pan: **Standard 12-cup muffin pan**

YOU WILL NEED:

Ingredients:

½ loaf of sourdough bread, cubed
1 ½ cups baked corn bread, cubed
1 stick butter
½ large onion, diced
1 cup mushroom, washed and
　　chopped
2 carrots, chopped
2 stalks celery, chopped

2 cloves garlic, minced
2 cups low sodium
　　chicken broth
¼ cup fresh parsley, chopped
1 tbsp fresh sage
1 tbsp fresh rosemary
½ lb ground sausage, cooked and
　　drained
2 eggs

Directions:

1. Preheat oven to 350°F and spray muffin pan.

2. When the oven is ready, bake the sourdough and corn bread cubes on a baking sheet for 25 minutes, or until toasted. Remove from oven and set aside.

3. In a large cast iron skillet, melt butter and sauté onions, mushroom, carrots, and celery until tender, about 10 minutes. Add garlic and cook for another minute. Pour in chicken broth and stir in parsley, sage, rosemary, and sausage.

4. In a large bowl, add bread cubes and slowly pour in the vegetable and broth mixture. Gently fold the mixture until all the bread cubes are coated. Season with salt and pepper to taste.

5. In a small bowl whisk the eggs and pour into the bread and vegetable mixture. Gently stir all the ingredients together.

6. Scoop the stuffing into the muffin cups. Press down firmly to help ensure they stay together. Divide the remaining stuffing among the cups.

7. Bake at 350°F for 20–25 minutes, until the tops are crisp and the muffins are set.

8. As long as the recipe contains at least 2 eggs, you can bake most stuffing recipes in the muffin pan.

BELLY UP TO
THE MINI MAC AND CHEESE BAR

I think this recipe epitomizes the beauty of the muffin pan. It is child-friendly, adorable, offers portion control, and is perfect for parties. Really all the things a muffin pan dish should be. And as an added bonus, this is not just a muffin pan recipe! For instructions and suggestions on how to set up your own Mac and Cheese Bar, see p. 232.

***Pan:* 2 mini 24-cup or 2 standard 12-cup muffin pans**

YOU WILL NEED:

Ingredients:

½ lb elbow macaroni

2 unsalted butter, plus more for pan

2 tbsp flour

¾ cup milk, room temp

1 ½ cups cheese, shredded

¼ cup Parmesan cheese, grated

2 egg yolks

¼ tsp paprika

Salt and pepper, to taste

Panko bread crumbs

Directions:

1. Preheat oven to 425°F and coat the cups of the muffin pan with butter.

2. In a large pasta pot, bring enough salted water to cover the pasta to a boil. Cook the macaroni until almost al dente, about 5 minutes. Check package directions and adjust 2–3 minutes less than package suggests for al dente. Drain and rinse under cold water to stop any further cooking. Set pasta aside.

3. In a large saucepan, melt butter over medium heat. Whisk in the flour and cook until the flour turns light brown, 1–2 minutes. Add in milk and whisk continuously until the mixture is smooth and comes to a boil, about 5 minutes. Add the cheeses and stir until melted.

4. Remove the pan from the heat and whisk in egg yolks and paprika.

5. Fold the cooked pasta into the cheese sauce. Add pepper if desired but do use plenty of salt to season this dish.

Tip: *When choosing cheese for your dish, try sticking with cheeses that melt really well. Cheddar, Jack, Swiss, Gruyere, and even American are great. I prefer to use a sharp aged cheddar when I make these mac and cheese bites. If you have some strong cheeses on hand like blue cheese or feta, mix in a small amount, about ¼ cup with a more neutral cheese like Jack so as to not overpower the dish. However, if you are anything like my Aunt Judy, just throw in whatever cheese you have in the cheese drawer and bake it up. It always works for her!*

6. If you are going to add any extra ingredients to the macaroni, now is the time to add it in.

7. Fill each muffin cup to the top, packing the noodles down gently.

8. Sprinkle the tops with panko crumbs and some more parmesan cheese.

9. Bake for 10 minutes, or until golden brown and bubbly.

10. Allow the trays to cool for 5 minutes before removing the macaroni cups from the pan. Use a butter knife to loosen the macaroni bites and place on a platter. Serve warm.

Tip: *You can make these bites ahead by following all the steps up until baking and place, covered, in the fridge until you are ready to bake. Or you can cook the mac and cheese bites ahead of time and store them in the fridge. When you are ready to use, preheat the oven to 400°F, place bites on a cooking sheet, and bake for 5 minutes, or until warm in the middle.*

MINI GOBBLER PIE WITH ROSEMARY GOAT CHEESE PESTO

Do you know what's better than Thanksgiving dinner? Thanksgiving leftovers! My family has a great tradition of having a leftovers party the evening after Thanksgiving. True to myself, I usually take a couple dishes and create a muffin pan dish using leftovers for the party. This is a fun night to share food and family traditions with friends. We have some amazing family friends who never fail to impress with their leftovers. At the end of the night, we send everyone home with more food, only now it's something new and exciting from someone else's family table.

Pan: Standard 12-cup muffin pan

YOU WILL NEED:

Ingredients:
6 uncooked biscuits, cut lengthwise
1 cup turkey, cubed
1 cup mashed potatoes

Rosemary Goat Cheese Pesto
⅓ cup of fresh rosemary
⅓ cup goat cheese, softened at
    room temperature
1 ½ cups of fresh parsley
2 garlic cloves
½ cup pine nuts
½ cup olive oil
½ cup cranberry sauce

Directions:

1. Preheat the oven to 375°F and grease a standard 12 cup muffin pan.

2. In a food processor or using a whisk and a mixing bowl, add all the ingredients for the pesto.

3. Slice each biscuit lengthwise. You should have 12 slices in total. Place each slice of biscuit in the well of muffin pan. Use a tart shaper or bottom of a shot glass to press the dough into the muffin cup.

4. Start by adding turkey pieces to the biscuit cup, followed by goat cheese pesto and finally topped with mashed potatoes.

5. Bake for 18 minutes or until the edges begin to turn golden brown. Remove and top with cranberry sauce.

Mix It Up: *There are plenty of other Thanksgiving leftovers that would make good additions to these mini gobbler pies. Try adding a veggie like green beans to the pie. Whatever the addition, make sure the final layer is potato.*

BBQ CHICKEN PIZZA CUPS

One of my favorite types of pizza is BBQ chicken. I like the combination of textures, flavors and colors. But really, anyway you press it out, roll it up, top it or slice it, I just love pizza. That's why this recipe is so great for all pizza lovers. Choose the toppings you prefer or better yet, get the family or guests involved and let everyone choose their own toppings. Use a separate muffin pan to display topping options, like in the Belly Up to the Mac & Cheese Bar recipe on p. 145.

Pan: **2 Standard 12-Cup muffin pans**

YOU WILL NEED:

Ingredients:
1 (13.8 oz) refrigerated pizza dough
1 cup cooked chicken, chopped
½ cup barbecue sauce
1 ½ cups mozzarella, shredded
¼ red onion, cut into strips
Cilantro, chopped

Directions:

1. Preheat oven to 400°F and spray 2 standard muffin pans.
2. Leaving the pizza dough rolled up like a log, slice into 16 rounds. Place the rounds in the cups and bake for 8 minutes.
3. While it bakes, mix together chicken and barbecue sauce in a bowl.
4. Remove from oven and press dough down. Divide chicken and onions among the 16 cups. Top with cheese.
5. Place muffin pan back in the oven and bake for an additional 15–18 minutes, or until the cheese is bubbly.
6. Top with cilantro and serve warm.

MINI LOUISIANA CORN DOGS WITH CAJUN KETCHUP

This is the corn dog . . . all grown up! Playing on the flavors of New Orleans cuisine, this recipe is sure to be a hit at any Mardi Gras party. This dish can be served as either an appetizer or main course.

***Pan:* Standard 12-cup muffin pan**

YOU WILL NEED:

Ingredients:

4 Andouille sausages, sliced into 16 pieces
1 large onion, chopped
1 bell pepper, chopped
1 box (8.5oz) cornbread mix
1 egg
⅓ cup buttermilk
1 tbsp Cajun or creole seasoning
1 cup ketchup
1 tbsp Dijon mustard
½ tsp hot sauce
1 tsp Cajun seasoning

Directions:

1. Preheat oven to 400°F and grease muffin pan.
2. In a large cast iron skillet, heat a tablespoon of oil over medium high heat. Cook onions, sausage, and peppers until vegetables are tender and sausage is browned. With a pair of tongs, remove the 16 pieces of sausage and place them aside.
3. In a bowl, mix together cornbread mix, egg, buttermilk and creole seasoning. When fully combined, add onion and peppers to the cornbread mixture. Stir until fully combined.
4. Spoon cornbread mixture into the muffin cups, filling them half way. In the center of each cup, place a piece of sausage.
5. Bake for 15–18 minutes, or until the edges begin to brown.
6. While it bakes, mix together ketchup, mustard, hot sauce, and seasoning. Serve sauce with corn dogs.

CITRUS SHRIMP TACO SALAD WITH CREAMY CILANTRO DRESSING

Chill out with this light, refreshing salad cup. Great for warm summer nights.

Pan: Jumbo 6-cup muffin pan

YOU WILL NEED:

Ingredients:
6 (8 in) flour or whole wheat
   tortillas
1 cup quinoa, uncooked
2 cups water
1 ½ cup of frozen corn
¼ tsp chili powder
½ lb shrimp
1 tbsp lemon pepper
⅛ tsp salt
1 cup cherry tomatoes

Arugula or greens of your choice
Fresh crumbly cheese like cotija
   or feta

Cilantro dressing:
1 cup of cilantro, stems removed
½ cup greek yogurt
2 cloves garlic
1 lime, juiced
¼ cup olive oil
1–2 tbsp apple cider vinegar

Directions:

1. Preheat the oven to 350°F and lightly grease a jumbo muffin pan.

2. Place one tortilla into each of the 6 jumbo muffin cups. You may need to overlap one side or two to make it fit.

3. Bake for 10–12 minutes.

4. Meanwhile, cook quinoa and corn. In a fine mesh strainer, rinse the quinoa with cold water. Rub the quinoa to remove quinoas coating, called saponin. It has a bitter taste. If the package says "pre-rinsed" you can skip this step. Drizzle a tsp of olive oil in a saucepan over medium high heat. Add quinoa and toast quinoa for about 1 minute, stirring, until all the water has evaporated.

5. Add 2 cups of water and bring the pan to a boil.

6. Turn the heat down to the lowest setting and cook, covered, for 15 minutes.

7. Remove the tortillas from the oven after 10–12 minutes or when the tortillas hold their shape and are golden brown around the edges.

8. While the quinoa cooks, heat tablespoon of oil in a large skillet over medium high heat. Add corn and cook 10 minutes or until the corn begins to brown, stirring occasionally. Stir in chili powder and remove from heat. Pour into a serving dish or Tupperware container. Wipe pan clean so it can be used for the shrimp.

9. After 15 minutes, remove the pan with quinoa from the heat and let stand for an additional 5 minutes, still covered. After 5 minutes, fluff the quinoa with a fork.

10. In small bowl, toss shrimp, 2 tablespoons of oil and 1 tablespoon of lemon pepper. Add shrimp to pan and cook until they are pink and curled up, 3–4 minutes. Remove from heat.

11. Finally, in a blender or food processor, combine cilantro, yogurt, garlic cloves, lime juice, and salt. While the mixture is blending, slowly add oil and vinegar until emulsified or has a smooth, creamy texture.

12. Build your salad: To the tortilla cup, add arugula, quinoa, corn, tomatoes, shrimp, fresh crumbled cheese, dressing and salt and pepper to taste.

Mix It Up: *If you have the grill going, why not try BBQ'ing the shrimp? Place lemon peppered shrimp on metal or soaked wooden skewer and grill over medium-high heat. Cook for about 2–3 minutes per side.*

INDIVIDUAL CHICKEN ALFREDO LASAGNA

Muffin pan lasagna is a great go-to meal. I like to serve one of the lasagna cups with a side salad and call it dinner.

Pan: 2 jumbo 6-cup muffin pans

YOU WILL NEED:

Ingredients:

2 cups chicken, shredded or cubed
2 cups Alfredo sauce
1 cup onion, chopped
1 tbsp chopped garlic
2 cups ricotta cheese (or 1 425g container)
1 large egg

½ cup grated Parmesan
4 strips bacon, cooked and crumbled
2 tbsp parsley, chopped
3 cups mozzarella cheese, grated
Wonton or potsticker wrappers

Directions:

1. Preheat oven to 375°F and lightly grease two jumbo 6-cup muffin pans (12 wells total).

2. Heat olive oil in a frying pan over medium heat. Add chopped onion and sauté until softened, about 3 minutes. Add chopped garlic and sauté for 1 minute more. Pour in alfredo sauce and chicken. Stir the pan, coating the chicken in the alfredo sauce. Remove from heat and set aside.

3. In a mixing bowl, combine ricotta cheese, egg, grated Parmesan, bacon and chopped parsley. Season well with salt and pepper.

4. Press one wonton wrapper into the bottom of the muffin cup. To create a base, add a pinch of the mozzarella cheese and then another won ton wrapper. This creates a sturdy base to start layering. Spoon a tablespoon of the chicken alfredo sauce on top of the wonton cup, next a tsp of the ricotta mixture, followed by a tablespoon of mozzarella and then topped with a wonton wrapper. Repeat the layering: chicken alfredo sauce, ricotta mixture, mozzarella cheese, wonton wrapper. When you have reached the top of the muffin cup, top the final won ton wrapper with just cheese.

5. Bake uncovered for 20 minutes or until sauce is bubbling and cheese is melted. If the edges begin to brown quicker than the cheese is melting, move tray to a lower rack.

6. Let the dish stand for 5 minutes before removing from the tray to allow the filling to firm up.

CHICKEN
MARSALA POT PIE

This is my version of chicken pot pie in the muffin pan with a marsala twist. It's very rich but oh so delicious.

Pan: Jumbo 6-cup muffin pan

YOU WILL NEED:

Ingredients:
2 refrigerated pie crusts
2 large chicken breasts, skinless and
    boneless
½ cup flour
Salt and pepper, to taste
2 tbsp butter
4 large shallots, chopped
1 tbsp rosemary leaves, finely chopped

2 garlic cloves, minced
8 oz mushrooms, cleaned and sliced
2 tbsp tomato paste
½ cup sweet marsala wine
¼ cup chicken stock
¼ cup sherry or dry white wine
2 tbsp heavy cream
1 egg, whisked

Directions:

1. Preheat oven to 425°F and grease a jumbo muffin pan including the top.
2. Split each chicken breast lengthwise to make two pieces. On a plate or in a zip top bag, combine flour, salt and pepper and dredge each piece of chicken.
3. In a large skillet, heat a tablespoon or two of olive oil and cook the pieces of chicken over medium heat for 1–2 minutes, or until browned on each side. You may need to do the chicken in batches. Once the chicken is cooked, remove from the pan and allow to rest before cutting into bite sized pieces.
4. In the same pan, add butter, shallots, rosemary and garlic. Cook for 5–6 minutes until shallots are tender. Return the chicken to the pan and with it the sliced mushrooms. Continue to cook for an additional 2–3 minutes. Add the tomato paste, marsala wine, stock, sherry, and cream.
5. Turn the heat down to low or simmer and allow the ingredients to cook down until the mixture is thickened, about 5 minutes, or until the chicken is completely cooked through.
6. While the sauce is thickening, prepare the crust.
7. Roll out each pie crust and cut each into 6 pieces, eyeballing the size so that each is generally the same size. If you'd like to make the pies look uniform in shape, cut dough with a large biscuit cutter.
8. Press each piece into each jumbo muffin cup. Allow the crust to peak up over the edges. Fill the cups with the chicken marsala mixture. Place the remaining 6 pieces of dough on top of the filling and press together with the dough from the bottom.
9. Make a slit in the center of the pie dough to vent. Brush with egg and sprinkle with salt.
10. Bake, covered for 20 minutes. Uncover and bake for an additional 10 minutes until nice and brown.

EMPADINHA DE POLLO

My family loves to travel. One year for New Years, we visited Rio de Janiero, Brazil for their big New Years party. It was an amazing experience. We traveled around with family friends who grew up in Brazil so we got to do so much of what the locals did. She took us to the best places to eat and we tried all kinds of food. This recipe is inspired by that trip.

Pan: Standard 12-cup muffin pan

Ingredients:

YOU WILL NEED:

Empindinha Dough:
4 cup all purpose flour, plus 6 tbsp
2 eggs
1 egg yolk
1 tsp of baking powder
4–5 tsp of cold water
Pinch of salt

Filling:
1 (14.5 oz) can hearts of palm, drained
1 ½ cups rotisserie chicken, shredded
2 tomatoes, chopped
2 big tomatoes, chopped
½ cup chopped olives
1 (15 oz) can of peas
2 tbsp of chopped onions
1 clove garlic, minced
1 tbsp cornstarch
1 cup of milk
2 tbsp of chopped parsley
3 tbsp of olive oil
Salt and pepper to taste

Directions:

1. Preheat the oven to 350°F and grease 1 standard muffin pan.
2. In a large bowl combine the eggs and egg yolk with the flour, butter, baking soda, and salt.
3. Using your hands, mix the ingredients together until well combined, for several minutes. Add the cold water to the dough and knead just until the desired dough-like consistency is reached. Try not to over knead the dough. Roll the dough into a large ball, place back into the bowl, cover and allow to rest in the fridge.
4. While the dough rests, heat 2 tablespoons of olive oil in a large pan over medium heat and cook the onions and garlic. Once the onions are translucent, add the heart of palm, tomato, olives, and peas. Cook for about 8 minutes.
5. In a bowl whisk the milk and cornstarch together and pour it until the pan with the vegetables and mix until the mixture thickens. Allow the mixture to come to a bubble and then turn off the heat.
6. Roll out the pastry dough and cut into 12 circles and place into the wells of the muffin pan. Press the dough into the pan.
7. Spoon about 1 ½ tbsps of filling into each cup. Cut another 12 circles and place on top of each cup. Pinch around the edges to create a seal.
8. Bake for 25 minutes.

KING RANCH CASSEROLE CUPS

If you love tortilla casseroles as much as I do, you need to try these casserole cups. A muffin sized twist on the popular Texas dish, these cups are great for packing in a lunch or bringing to a potluck.

Pan: Jumbo 6-cup muffin pan

YOU WILL NEED:

Ingredients:

12 corn tortillas
3 tbsp olive oil
½ medium size onion, chopped
⅓ red bell pepper, chopped
2 large clove garlic, crushed
1 medium poblano pepper, roasted, peeled and chopped
3 tbsp all-purpose flour
1 cup whole milk or heavy cream
1 cup chicken broth
1 (10 oz) can diced tomatoes and green chiles
1 tsp cilantro, chopped
2 cups cheddar cheese, shredded
3 cups cooked chicken, shredded
Salt and pepper, to taste

Directions:

1. Preheat oven to 350°F and spray a jumbo muffin pan.

2. Separate 6 corn tortillas and place in the microwave, wrapped in a barely damp paper towel, for 30 seconds. This will make them more pliable. Gently place one tortilla in each muffin cup and press into the bottom. Cut the remaining 6 tortillas into small squares and set aside.

3. In a large skillet, heat olive oil over medium high heat. To the pan add onions and bell pepper and sauté until soft. Add garlic and poblano and cook a minute longer.

4. Sprinkle flour over the vegetables and stir to coat. Reduce to medium heat.

5. While the vegetables are cooking, whisk together milk, broth, tomatoes, and chiles. Pour the milk mixture into the skillet and stir together. Add tortilla squares, chicken and one cup of cheese into the pan. Give the whole mixture another stir.

6. Turn the heat back up to medium high to bring the mixture to a simmer. Continue to stir the sauce until it becomes thick and bubbly. Once the mixture is thick, Stir in cilantro and remove from heat.

7. Scoop a generous amount of the chicken tortilla mixture into the tortilla cups. Top with the remaining cup of cheese.

8. Bake for 20–25 minutes, or until tortillas are crispy and the cheese is bubbly. Serve warm.

LIGHTENED-UP MINI CHEESEBURGER PIE

While I was in grad school, my roommate Lisa used to make this fantastic cheeseburger pie. We would sit in front of the TV, eat cheeseburger pie and watch reruns of our favorite shows. This is a mini version of that recipe.

***Pan:* Jumbo 6-cup muffin pan**

YOU WILL NEED:

Ingredients:

1lb ground turkey
1 tbsp olive oil
½ onion, chopped
3 cloves of garlic, minced
1 tbsp Worcestershire sauce
2 ¼ cups Heart Healthy Bisquik

¾ cup water
1 egg
1 cup non-fat cottage cheese
¾ cup shredded 2% cheddar cheese
1 large tomato, sliced

Directions:

1. Preheat oven to 350°F and grease a 6-cup jumbo muffin pan.

2. In a skillet over medium heat start to brown turkey, garlic, and onions.

3. While the meat cooks, in a large bowl, gradually add water to Bisquik. If the dough becomes too sticky, add more bisquik. Split the dough evenly among the bottom of the 6 cups. Press the dough firmly into the bottom and up the sides.

4. Once the dough is in place, return to the meat and add the Worcestershire sauce. Give it a mix. Cook until the meat is no longer pink. Remove the skillet from the heat and put to the side.

5. In a bowl mix together egg, cottage cheese, and meat mixture. Stir all the ingredients together.

6. Evenly spoon the ingredients on top of the dough. Top with cheese and a slice of tomato.

7. Bake for 20 minutes.

MINI ALBONDIGAS TORTAS WITH A ROASTED TOMATO CILANTRO DIPPING SAUCE

Here is a random tidbit about my Mama: Albondigas is her favorite Spanish word. She told me this several times during my years in Spanish class and it always made me giggle. It means meatball and it is terribly fun to say. Al-bon-digas. Al-bon-digas. Hopefully this dish also becomes a favorite.

Pan: 2 standard 12-cup muffin pans

YOU WILL NEED:

Ingredients:

1 Pillsbury French bread loaf can

8 precooked turkey or beef meatball halved

4 slices of pepper jack, quartered

½ avocado, cubed

Sauce

1 tbsp olive oil

1 (14.5 oz) can of fire roasted tomatoes

3 whole cloves of garlic, minced

½ onion, chopped

1 tbsp cumin

Handful or two of cilantro leaves

Directions:

1. Preheat the oven to 350°F and grease 2 standard muffin pans.

2. In a pan, heat olive oil over medium heat. Cook onions and garlic for about 2 minutes. In a blender, blend the tomatoes, cumin, and cilantro until the consistency of marinara sauce. Add the onions then garlic and give another quick blend.

3. Slice the loaf into 15 pieces. Press each slice into the muffin pan and press into the sides of the cup.

4. Par-bake the bread for about 6 minutes.

5. After 6 minutes, remove from the oven and carefully place half a meatball, cut side up, in the bread cup. Top with a quarter of cheese and return to the oven, this time on the lowest rack.

6. Allow it to cook for about 13–15 minutes.

7. Serve with roasted tomato sauce and a slice of avocado.

Party Time: *The green avocado, white bread, and red sauce make a great addition to any fiesta or Cinco de Mayo party.*

MINI BUREK

When I was researching for this book, I wanted to include dishes that showcased dishes from different countries. Burek is a popular dish in modern day Turkey, but many other countries have their own version of this dish. Traditionally it is filled with ground beef or sometimes with spinach and fresh cheese. I have adapted this simple dish for the muffin pan.

Pan: Standard 12-cup muffin pan

YOU WILL NEED:

Ingredients:

1 pkg phyllo pastry
1 lb ground beef or turkey
1 cup warm water
3 tbsp oil
½ tsp salt
1 small onions, finely chopped

1 tsp thyme
1 tbsp ground sage
1 tsp paprika
1 clove garlic, minced
Salt and pepper, to taste
Sour cream, as a topping

Directions:

1. Preheat oven to 400°F and spray a 12-cup muffin pan.

2. In a large frying pan, cook onions in oil until translucent. Add the ground meat and cook until no longer pink.

3. While the meat cooks, prepare the phyllo. In a small bowl, mix together warm water, oil, and salt. This will be used to keep phyllo from drying out, referred to as the cooking liquid.

4. When the meat has cooked, remove phyllo from the fridge. Working in batches of 3–4 sheets, sprinkle cooking liquid on the top most phyllo sheet. Add 3–4 tablespoons of meat to the long side of the phyllo, spreading it out into a line. Rolling away from you, roll meat side of the phyllo into a long tube. If the phyllo begins to break, add more liquid. Begin coiling phyllo like a snake and then cut along the snake, creating spiral discs of phyllo and meat. Place the disc flat into the muffin pan. The middle should reach the bottom while outer edges reach up the sides of the cup. Repeat this until all the cups are filled.

5. Cover with foil, and bake for 25 minutes. Remove from oven and remove foil. If there is leftover cooking liquid, divide it among the 12 cups. Return to the oven and bake for an additional 5 minutes.

6. Serve with sour cream.

MONTE CRISTO BITES

The first time I had a Monte Cristo sandwich I was on vacation with my family. I can't remember who ordered it off the room service menu, but I do remember loving it! I think it's where my love of sweet and savory started. Whenever I want to treat myself to a staycation, I bake up a batch of these puppies, curl up in a big comfy robe, and pop in a movie. Instant vacation.

***Pan:* 2 standard 12-cup muffin pans**

YOU WILL NEED:

Ingredients:
1 can butter flavored biscuits
6 slices of ham
6 slices of turkey

6 slices of swiss
6 slices of cheddar (or approx.
   1 cup shredded cheddar)
6 tbsp of raspberry jam

Directions:

1. Preheat the oven to 350°F and grease 2 standard muffin pans.
2. Spilt 8 of the biscuits in half lengthwise, creating 16 biscuit slices.
3. Layer one piece of ham, then turkey, followed by a slice of swiss and a slice of cheddar. Roll into a log. Cut the roll into 3 equal pieces.
4. Spread ½ tablespoon of jam on a slice of biscuit and place one piece of the roll in the center.
5. Stretch the edges of the biscuit over the filling and press the edges together at the top for a tight seal.
6. Press the biscuit in the dough into the muffin pan, seam side down.
7. Bake for 13–15 minutes, until the dough is a light golden brown.
8. Remove from the oven and allow to cool slightly. Plate the monte cristo bites and dust with powedered sugar. Serve with a side of extra raspberry jam.

Embrace Leftovers: *There will be ⅔ of a meat and cheese roll left when you have made all 16 bites. I say roll it up in a tortilla while you wait for these guys to bake or just eat it while you are working. Remember, these are your staycation treats and calories don't count while you are on vacation.*

NOT-SO-SLOPPY JOES

A "clean" twist on the original Sloppy Joe, this Not-So-Sloppy Joe is made with healthy ground turkey and packed with veggies.

Pan: **Standard 12-cup muffin pan**

YOU WILL NEED:

Ingredients:

1 can of biscuit dough
20 oz lean ground turkey
1 cup onion, finely chopped
1 cup shredded carrot
1 medium zucchini, chopped
1 large garlic clove, minced
¾ cup ketchup

1 tbsp tomato paste
½ cup water
4–5 squirts of Worcestershire sauce
1 tbsp brown sugar
½ tsp dry mustard
1 tsp chili powder
Hot sauce, to taste
Salt & pepper, to taste

Directions:

1. Preheat oven to 350°F and grease a standard muffin pan.

2. In a skillet over medium heat, sauté turkey until almost cooked through. Add onions, carrots, and garlic and continue to cook for 2–3 minutes. Finally add zucchini and cook for 2 additional minutes.

3. To the meat mixture add ketchup, tomato paste, water, Worcestershire sauce, sugar, mustard, chili powder, and hot sauce. Mix well and simmer for 15 minutes. Add salt and pepper to taste.

4. Cut off ⅓ of the biscuit dough from each round, press flat and set aside. Press the large piece of biscuit into each cup and up the sides of the well. Add a generous amount of filling to each dough cup. Cover each cup with the smaller piece of biscuit dough, sealing the bottom and the top biscuit pieces together as best you can.

5. Bake for 15 minutes, or until biscuit dough is golden brown.

PHILLY CHEESESTEAK BITES

Provolone or Cheez-Whiz? Try one batch of each! Either way, these cheesesteak bites are a little bit of Philly heaven.

***Pan:* Standard 12-cup muffin pan**

YOU WILL NEED:

Ingredients:

2 sheets of puff pastry, thawed
1 pkg (7 oz) of roast beef, thinly sliced
    into strips
1–2 tbsp olive oil
1 medium yellow onion, thinly sliced
8 oz mushrooms, sliced

1 tbsp minced garlic
1 bell pepper, seeded and thinly sliced
2 tsp Worcestershire sauce
6 slices of provolone or Velveeta slices
1 egg, beaten
Salt and pepper to taste

Directions:

1. Preheat oven to 400°F and grease one standard muffin pan.
2. Roll out the puff pastry, cutting each sheet into six pieces. Repeat with the second sheet. Place a piece of the puff pastry into each cup. Put the tray in the fridge to keep the dough cool.
3. In a large skillet, heat olive oil over medium heat. Add the bell pepper, onion, mushrooms, and minced garlic to the skillet. Saute until tender, about 3 minutes, taking care not to burn the garlic. Season with salt and pepper to taste.
4. In a large bowl, add sliced roast beef and worcestershire. With a fork, or your hands, toss the roast beef, coating it in the worcestershire. Add the veggies to the meat and give it once last mix.
5. Take the tray out of the fridge. Add half a piece of cheese to each puff pastry cup. Fill the puff pastry with ¼ cup of the meat and vegetable mix.
6. Fold the corners of the puff pastry towards the middle to enclose the filling.
7. Bake for 20 minutes, or until golden brown.

SPAGHETTI CARBONARA TWISTS-UP

This is my new favorite way to eat pasta, all twisted up.

***Pan:* Standard 12-cup muffin pan**

YOU WILL NEED:

Ingredients:
½ lb spaghetti or spaghettini
5 oz pancetta, cubed
¾ cup parmesan cheese, grated

3 eggs
½ cup heavy cream
Pepper to taste

Directions:

1. Preheat the oven to 375°F and grease one 12-cup muffin pan.

2. Cook the spaghetti in a pot of boiling, salted water until al dente. Drain and return to the pot.

3. While the pasta cooks, use a skillet to cook the pancetta over medium heat for about 5–6 minutes until the fat is rendered. Remove the pancetta with a slotted spoon and set aside on a plate with a paper towel.

4. Pour the fat from the pan into the spaghetti pot, add ½ cup of the parmesan to the pot as well as the pepper to taste.

5. Using a fork, grab a large scoop of pasta, place in the well of a muffin pan and give it a twist. Continue to twist until the spaghetti is nicely packed. The cup should be ½ full of spaghetti.

6. In a small bowl, beat the eggs and stir in the heavy cream. Evenly distribute the mixture into the 12 cups, about 1 tablespoon each. Top with the pancetta and remaining cheese.

7. Bake for 20 minutes, or until the edges begin to lightly brown.

SPICY THAI PEANUT CHICKEN ROLLS WITH CILANTRO YOGURT SAUCE

This is my take on the delicious flavors of Thai Peanut Chicken. Wrapped in bread, these rolls are great for lunches. The combination of spicy sriracha, sweet peanut butter, and salty soy sauce makes this dish stand out. Add a dollop of the yogurt sauce and your coworkers will start wonder where they can buy one too.

Pan: **Standard 12-cup muffin pan**

YOU WILL NEED:

Ingredients:
1 Pillsbury French loaf can
1 (6 oz) chicken breast, cooked and cubed
1–2 tbsp olive oil
2 tbsp soy sauce
1 tbsp peanut butter
1 tsp Sriracha or other chili sauce
1 cup mozzarella cheese, shredded
¼ cup matchstick carrots

¼ cup red onions, thinly sliced
2 tbsp unsalted peanuts, chopped
⅓ cup cilantro, chopped
¼ cup green onions, chopped

Cilantro Yogurt Sauce:
1 (6 oz) container or ½ cup Greek yogurt
⅓ cup cilantro, chopped
Juice of ½ a lime

Directions

1. Preheat the oven 350°F and grease your muffin pan.
2. In a small pan heat chicken in olive oil. Allow chicken to brown up for a minute or two. Meanwhile, combine soy sauce, peanut butter, and sriracha in a bowl and whisk. Pour the mixture over the chicken and stir to coat.
3. In a blender add the Greek yogurt and cilantro. Pulse until well combined. Pour into your serving container. Squeeze in the lime juice and stir to combine.
4. Unroll French bread loaf. First add a thin layer of the cilantro yogurt. Add a layer of mozzarella cheese, then chicken, followed by the carrots, onions, cilantro and green onions. Spread the mixture to the corners.
5. Starting from long side, gently roll the bread back into a loaf shape. To ensure smooth cuts, place the whole roll in the refrigerator for several minutes to firm up. Once it is firm, slice the roll into 12 equal slices.
6. Place each roll into the well of each muffin cup. Generously sprinkle the peanuts on top of each roll up.
7. Bake the whole tray for 15 minutes. Serve with the rest of the cilantro yogurt sauce.

TUNA MINI MELTS

The lemon and herbs in this tuna melt not only make for a very light, fresh sandwich but will also make your whole kitchen smell like summer. If you have a green thumb and garden with fresh herbs, use whatever you have growing. Substitutions are always okay, especially when you grew it yourself.

Pan: **Standard 6-cup muffin pan**

YOU WILL NEED:

Ingredients:

1 (12 oz) can white albacore tuna
Unsalted butter
⅓ cup mayonnaise
1 tsp Dijon mustard
½ small lemon, zested and juiced
3 tbsp fresh chives, chopped

2 tbsp fresh parsley, chopped
1 tsp fresh thyme, chopped
Freshly ground pepper, to taste
6 whole wheat English muffins
2 Roma tomatoes, sliced
12 slices of white cheddar (or cheese of your choice)

Directions:

1. Preheat oven to 375°F and grease a 6-cup standard muffin pan with butter.
2. In a bowl, combine the mayo, mustard, lemon, herbs, and pepper. Gently stir in the tuna, breaking it up slightly.
3. Firmly press a half of an English Muffin into the muffin cup.
4. Scoop a tablespoon of the tuna mixture into the English muffin cup. Top with a slice of tomato and a slice of cheese.
5. Bake at 375°F for 10 to 12 minutes or until cheese is bubbling and toasty brown.

MINI
GYROS

I couldn't resist creating a mini version of the gyro. The combination of textures and flavors is so wonderful. I could eat these everyday.

Pan: **Standard 12-cup muffin pan**

YOU WILL NEED:

Ingredients:
12 slices gyro meat, cut into 1 inch
    squares
2 sheets of lavash bread, cut into
    12 squares or 12 circles

Tzatziki Sauce
1 cup plain greek yogurt
½ cucumber, grated
1 clove of garlic, minced
½ tbsp fresh dill, finely
    chopped
½ tbsp olive oil
½ tsp lemon juice
½ tbsp red wine vinegar
1 ½ cup cherry tomatoes
Feta, crumbled

Directions:

1. Preheat the oven to 325°F and grease the muffin pan.

2. In a bowl, mix together the tzatziki ingredients and let it sit while you bake lavash cups.

3. Place a square or circle of lavash bread into each cup. Press the bread firmly into the bottom of the cup.

4. Bake for about 6–8 minutes or until the bread is hard and crispy like a cracker. Remove from the oven and let them cool.

5. Fill cups with pieces of gyro meat, a dollop of tzatziki, a cherry tomato, and some feta sprinkled on top Garnish with a slice of cucumber.

MINI BUFFALO CHICKEN MEATLOAF WITH CREAMY BLUE CHEESE MASHED POTATOES

I love getting random gifts from friends. Once a family friend gave me close to 30 bottles of buffalo wing sauce. I tried to think of as many recipes as I could to use the buffalo sauce. I ate a lot buffalo wings, a few buffalo chicken pizzas, a couple buffalo chicken salads, numerous buffalo chicken tacos, and one bowl of buffalo mashed potatoes. However, after several bottles of wing sauce, I had yet to think of a recipe for the muffin pan. Then it dawned on me: over the time I had worked on the blog I had so many suggestions for meatloaf in the muffin pan but I had yet to make one. So I decided to create a buffalo chicken meatloaf muffin. I pair it with blue cheese mashed potatoes.

Pan: **Standard 12-cup Muffin Pan**

YOU WILL NEED:

Ingredients:

1 ¼ lb ground chicken or turkey
1 cup plain panko breadcrumbs
⅓ cup (about 1 rib) celery, diced
⅓ cup crumbled blue cheese
¼ cup white onion, diced
½ cup milk
1 large egg

½ cup buffalo wing sauce
¼ tsp garlic powder
¼ tsp dried parsley
Pinch of black pepper
2 lbs potatoes, peeled and cubed
5 tbsp butter
1 ½ tsp salt
½ cup milk
4 tbsp blue cheese, crumbled

Directions:

1. Preheat oven to 350°F and grease muffin pan.
2. In a large bowl, mix meat, breadcrumbs, celery, blue cheese, and onion.
3. In a separate, smaller bowl, whisk together milk, egg, wing sauce, garlic powder, parsley, and pepper.
4. Pour wet ingredients into meat mixture and combine.
5. Divide mixture among the 12 cups.
6. Bake for 30 minutes.
7. While the meatloaf muffins bake, prepare the mashed potatoes.
8. In a large pot of water, cook potatoes until fork tender. In a stand mixer, beat the potatoes, butter, blue cheese, and salt. Slowly add milk until creamy.
9. Remove meatloaf muffins from the oven and allow to cool slightly. Serve with mashed potatoes.

Look At That! *For a fun look, try piping the mashed potatoes on top like frosting on a cupcake. Place mashed potatoes in a large zip top bag. Cut a corner of the bag and pipe the mashed potatoes on top of the muffins like frosting.*

MINI
FISH TACOS

San Diego is known for their delicious fish tacos. You could say it is our signature dish, like San Francisco chiopino or Philly cheesesteaks. And like other cities with signature dishes, everyone has an idea of where to find the best version. I say the best fish tacos in town are the ones you make at home . . . especially if you make them in your muffin pan.

Pan: Standard 12-cup muffin pan

YOU WILL NEED:

Ingredients:

12 white corn tortillas
2 tilapia filets
¼ tsp garlic powder
½ tsp paprika
½ tsp ground coriander
¼ tsp salt

4 seeded jalepenos
½ cup sour cream
1 cup cilantro
1 clove garlic
1 lime, juiced
1 tbsp olive oil
1 cup red cabbage

Directions:

1. Preheat oven to 350°F and grease muffin pan and a baking sheet.
2. Cover the tortillas in a damp paper towel and heat in the microwave for 30 seconds. This makes them more pliable. Cut the tortillas in a square or circle. Save the edges for another recipe.
3. When the oven is ready, place each tortilla square in the well of the muffin pan.
4. Bake for 15–20 minutes until they are nice and crispy.
5. Combine the garlic, paprika, coriander, and salt in a small bowl. Rub both sides of the fish with the spice mixture. Place fish on greased baking sheet.
6. Put the fish in the oven with the tortillas and bake for 10–12 minutes, until the fish is flakey and the tortillas are ready.
7. While the fish bakes, prepare the sauce. In a blender, combine jalepenos, sour cream, cilantro, garlic, lime juice. Blend well. With the blender still on, open the top and pour olive oil in to the blender in a steady stream.
8. Remove both the tortilla cups and fish from the oven when finished. Allow the tortillas to cool on a rack. Chop fish and divide among the tortilla cups. Top the fish with the cabbage and then the jalapeño cream sauce. Garnish with lime and cilantro.

Dessert

APPLE PIE ROSES WITH A CHEDDAR CHEESE CRUST

These apple pie roses are almost too beautiful to eat. Almost. With the added cheddar to the crust, I could hardly keep my hands off of them.

Pan: Standard 12-cup muffin pan

YOU WILL NEED:

Ingredients:
1 box (2 rolls) pie crust
4 apples, thinly sliced
4 cups water
½ cup granulated sugar

¼ cup lemon juice
¼ cup brown sugar
1 ½ tsp cinnamon
½ tsp nutmeg
½ cup cheddar, shredded

Directions:

1. Preheat oven to 425°F and lightly grease a standard muffin pan.

2. In a large saucepot, bring the water, sugar, and lemon juice to a boil. Thinly slice the apples (approx. 24 slices per apple) and add to the pot. Allow apples to boil for 2–4 minutes depending on thickness. The apples should be flexible but not falling apart.

3. Drain the apples and allow them to dry on a rack or paper towel while you prepare the crust.

4. Take the piecrusts out of the fridge and let them reach just slightly cooler than room temperature.

5. In a small bowl mix together the brown sugar, cinnamon, nutmeg and cheese. Evenly divide the mixture between both crusts. Gently press all the toppings into the crust.

6. Slice each crust into 7 thin strips. The end strips are shorter so they should be combined to create one strip, leaving you with 6 slices in total.

7. Place approximately 8 slices of apple, overlapping the ends, onto each strip of crust. The rounded edge of the apple should be peaking out over the edge of the crust. The more apple off the crust, the bigger the apple "blooms."

8. Rolling away from you, roll each strip into a tight coil. Admire your handy work before placing each rose into the well of the muffin pan. If your dough is starting to get too sticky, place it back in the fridge for a minute or two until it firms up.

9. Once you have rolled up all 12 roses, cover in foil.

10. Bake at 425°F for 15 minutes. Remove the foil and bake for another 15 minutes making it 30 minutes total baking time. Keep an eye on your buds; if the edges begin to get too brown, cover back up with foil.

11. When they are browned up nicely, take the tray from the oven and run knife around the edges to loosen the crust. Serve them on the platter or next a big scoop of ice cream.

LEMON BASIL RICOTTA CAKES WITH GLAZED BLUEBERRIES

The lemon, basil, and blueberries make this appetizer great for a summer party.

***Pan:* Mini 24-cup muffin pan**

YOU WILL NEED:

Ingredients:
2 cups (30 oz) Whole Milk Ricotta
2 eggs
4 tbsp basil leaves, chopped
2 lemons, juiced
Zest of 1 lemon

Blueberry Glaze:
6 oz blueberries
½ cup powdered sugar
¼ cup water
¼ cup lemon

Directions:

1. Preheat oven to 350°F and grease a mini muffin pan.

2. In a medium size bowl, mix the ricotta, eggs, basil, lemon juice, and lemon zest. Spoon the ricotta mixture onto the top of each cup. The mixture will shrink a bit in the oven.

3. Bake in the oven for 15–17 minutes or until the sides of the bites begin to pull away from the pan.

4. Meanwhile, place the blueberries, sugar, water, and lemon in a small saucepan. Heat over medium high heat until the sauce begins to boil. Turn down to low heat and allow to simmer. The longer the blueberries stay in the more they begin to break down. For intact berries only leave them in the pot for 3–4 minutes. Allow 8–10 minutes for softer, more jam-like blueberries.

5. Once the ricotta has cooled, run a sharp knife around the edge and flip the pan onto a large platter or the backside of baking tray.

6. You choose: Place blueberries on top and serve as is, or place cover with blueberries and set in the refrigerator for a more solid glaze.

PUMPKIN SNICKERDOODLE TREATS WITH BUTTERSCOTCH GLAZE

I built this recipe around my love for all things pumpkin.

Pan: **Standard 12-cup muffin pan**

YOU WILL NEED:

Ingredients:

5 cups crispy rice cereal
3 tbsp unsalted butter
1 cup canned pumpkin puree
1 (10 oz) bag mini marshmallows
½ tsp pure vanilla extract
1 tsp cinnamon

¼ tsp nutmeg
⅛ tsp ground cloves
⅛ tsp salt

Butterscotch Glaze

½ cup butterscotch (or caramel) chips
3 tbsp heavy cream

Directions:

1. Spray down a 24-cup mini muffin pan.

2. In a sauce pan, cook pumpkin puree for 5–6 minutes. The pumpkin will caramelize and reduce down to about a ¼ cup to ⅓ cup. In a separate large skillet, cook butter until it gives off a nutty aroma. Add pumpkin puree to the butter, as well as the vanilla, cinnamon, nutmeg, cloves, and salt. Fold in marshmallows. Stir until melted. Remove from heat.

3. Let the marshmallow mixture sit until it reaches room temperature. When it has, stir in cereal.

4. Using a cookie scoop, fill each muffin cup with cereal mixture, patting it down with a spatula until the wells are tightly packed.

5. Allow the tray to set for 25–30 minutes before removing.

6. While the tray sets, mix up the butterscotch glaze. Combine the butterscotch chips and cream in a microwave safe bowl. Microwave in 30 second intervals until melted.

7. Dip or drizzle butterscotch topping on pumpkin cereal cups.

SALTED DARK CHOCOLATE CARAMEL PEANUT BUTTER CUPS

My goodness gracious! Not only are these peanut butter cups easy to make, they get a grown up twist by using dark chocolate and filling them with peanut butter AND caramel.

***Pan:* 2 standard 12-cup silicone muffin pans or 1 mini 24-cup silicone muffin pan**

YOU WILL NEED:

Ingredients:
1 cup peanut butter
¼ cup powdered sugar

10 oz dark chocolate
¼ cup caramel sauce
Sea salt

Directions:

1. In a bowl, combine peanut butter and powdered sugar, mixing together until smooth. Place in the fridge while you melt the chocolate.

2. To prepare the chocolate, pour chips into a microwave safe bowl and heat for 30-second intervals. Stir in between each 30 seconds until the chocolate is fully melted.

3. Spoon a tsp or so of chocolate into each cup, taking care to cover the entire bottom and up the sides. The more chocolate on the bottom of the cup, the easier it is to remove. Place in the refrigerator for about 10 minutes, or until the chocolate has set.

4. Fill the chocolate cup about ⅔ the way with the peanut butter mixture. Top with a small amount of caramel sauce until the cup is ¾ full.

5. Finally pour the chocolate over the top of the cup until full. Sprinkle the chocolate with some flakes of sea salt. Return to the fridge for an additional 10 minutes.

Party Time: *Keep the tray you plan to serve the peanut butter cups in the fridge or freezer until it is time to plate. That will help the chocolate from melting before people have had a chance to enjoy it.*

GOLDEN S'MORE BLONDIE BITES

Who wants s'more blondies?

***Pan:** Standard 12-cup muffin pan*

YOU WILL NEED:

Ingredients:

½ cup unsalted butter (1 stick), melted
1 large egg
1 cup light brown sugar, packed
1 tbsp vanilla extract
1 cup all-purpose flour
3–3 ½ cups of graham cracker cereal
1 cup mini marshmallows
1 cup chocolate chips

Directions:

1. Preheat even to 350°F and spray a standard muffin pan.

2. In a large bowl whisk together egg, brown sugar, and vanilla. When the butter has cooled slightly, add it to the bowl and continue to whisk until smooth. Add the flour and stir just until combined, taking care not to overmix.

3. Fold in graham cracker cereal, marshmallows, and chocolate chips with a rubber spatula.

4. Scoop the batter into the muffin cups and press down firmly into the bottom.

5. Bake at 350°F for 18–20 minutes, or until the bars have set and middle is firm.

6. Allow at least 30 minutes for the cups to cool before removing from the muffin pan.

Mix It Up: *I really like using a really dark chocolate for this recipe because I feel it balances out all the sugar. Semisweet and bittersweet chocolate chips work as well. And if you have a serious sweet tooth, try white chocolate or butterscotch chips!*

TURTLE BROWNIE BITES

Brownies and caramel and pecans, oh my!

Pan: Mini 24-cup muffin pan

YOU WILL NEED:

Ingredients:
½ cup unsalted butter, melted
1 cup granulated sugar
⅔ cup unsweetened cocoa powder
2 eggs
2 tsp vanilla extract
1 tbsp brewed coffee or water

¼ tsp salt
½ cup all purpose flour
¼ cup pecans,
     finely chopped
1 bag soft chocolate covered
     caramel candies
Caramel topping

Directions:

1. Preheat oven to 350°F and spray and lightly flour a mini muffin pan.

2. In a bowl, mix together butter, sugar, and cocoa powder. Stir in eggs, vanilla, coffee or water, and salt. Gradually pour in flour and mix until well incorporated.

3. Scoop about 1 tablespoon of batter into each muffin cup. Sprinkle the chopped pecans on top of the brownie batter.

4. Bake at 350°F for 9–12 minutes, or until the brownies begin to pull away from the sides.

5. Remove from the oven and immediately press one piece of chocolate caramel candy in the top of each brownie bite.

6. Allow the brownies to cool completely before removing from the pan. Run a knife around th edge of the cup to help loosen the brownie.

7. Top the turtle brownie bites with a caramel drizzle and serve.

Tip: *Store in an airtight container at room temperature. They can be frozen for up to 3 months.*

ORANGE AND CRANBERRY WHITE CHOCOLATE BUTTONS

Orange and cranberry are such a festive combination. I like to serve these little treats around the holidays. A special thanks to my dear friend Deanna for helping me with this recipe.

Pan: **Mini 24-cup silicone muffin pan**

YOU WILL NEED:

Ingredients:
10 oz white chocolate
½ tsp shortening
¼ tsp orange extract
Pinch of salt

2 tbsp cranberries, chopped
Zest of one small orange
Pinch of sugar
2 tbsp candied ginger, chopped

Directions:

1. Mix white chocolate with the shortening and orange extract. Add a pinch of salt and heat in a microwave safe bowl at 50% at 1 minute intervals. Mix until smooth.

2. While the chocolate is in the microwave, add a pinch of sugar to a cutting board to mince the orange zest. Combine zest, cranberry, and ginger in small bowl.

3. Scoop a tablespoon of white chocolate into the bottom of each cup. Top the chocolate with the cranberry ginger mixture.

4. Place the tray in the freezer for 30–60 minutes or overnight.

5. Pop the chocolate out of tray and serve.

CHOCOLATE BANANA CREAM PUDDING CUPS

Aren't these beautiful? They are impressive looking but really easy to assemble. They would make a great addition to a bridal or baby shower.

Pan: Mini 24-cup muffin pan

YOU WILL NEED:

Ingredients:

1 (3.4 oz) pkg banana cream instant pudding
2 cups milk
1 pkg dark chocolate cookie dough
¼ cup heavy whipping cream
1 tsp vanilla extract
1 banana
Vanilla wafers
½ cup dark chocolate chips

Directions:

1. Preheat oven to 350°F and spray a mini muffin pan.

2. Divide chocolate cookie dough into 24 equal pieces and roll into balls. Place one ball of cookie dough into each muffin cup.

3. Bake for 13–15 minutes.

4. While cookie dough bakes, prepare the banana pudding and whipped cream. In a large bowl, add one package of banana pudding to 2 cups of cold milk. Whisk until combined. Place in refrigerator for 5 minutes.

5. In a food processor with a whipping blade or in a stand mixer with a whisk, whip heavy cream and vanilla until it forms stiff peaks.

6. When the chocolate cookie cups are finished, remove from oven and allow to cool on a rack. The cups should start to sink in the middle. With the handle of a wooden spoon or your thumb (when it has cooled enough), press the divot even further to create a well for the pudding.

7. When the pudding is set, spoon a tsp of it into the cookie cups. Scoop the whipped cream into a zip top bag, cutting a corner off to pipe the whipped cream on top of the pudding. Place one vanilla wafer in the pudding.

8. Slice a banana very thin into 24 slices. Decorate with the banana and chocolate chips.

BLUEBERRY COCONUT POPSICLES

For the first 3 years I lived in San Diego, I had no air conditioning in my house or my car. Summers were tough. I was warm a lot. To help beat the heat, I drank a lot of smoothies. I'd love to say it was because they are full of good-for-you stuff but really it was because they were cold and easy to make. Eventually I started making popsicles out of the smoothies to save for a quick dessert on those "85°F at 9 p.m." evenings.

Pan: Mini 12-cup silicone muffin pan

YOU WILL NEED:

Ingredients:
1 cup of frozen blueberries
½ cup of plain greek yogurt
½ cup of coconut milk
¼ cup sweetened shredded coconut
1–2 tbsp of sugar or honey

Directions:

1. In a blender, combine yogurt and coconut milk. Blend until smooth. Add blueberries and shredded coconut and puree.

2. Add one tablespoon of sugar and blend. Taste to see if it needs additional sweeteners.

3. Pour the smoothie mixture into the muffin cups, filling ¾ of the way to the top. Cover the muffin pan with a sheet of foil. Press the foil to the muffin pan to trace the outline of muffin cups. Make a small cut in the center with a sharp knife. Using a popsicle stick or plastic spoon press through slit in the foil.

4. Freeze the tray for 4 hours or overnight.

STRAWBERRY CHOCOLATE HAZELNUT PULL-APART MUFFINS

I like food that is fun to eat and fun to look at. When I was a kid my family would attend a brunch every New Years Day that was all about playing with your food. It was called the Football Bagel Breakfast. Our friends would bring the most creative dishes. There was even a prize at this brunch for the best presentation. My favorites over the years include a football stadium made out of bagels and cream cheese, the iceberg made out of cream cheese, covered in black olive penguins, with a small scale replica of the Titanic crashed into it and a world map made out of peas. Food should always be fun, that's why I like this dish so much. Pull apart bread is just so fun to eat.

Pan: Standard 12-cup muffin pan

YOU WILL NEED:

Ingredients:

1 tube of refrigerated French bread dough

⅔ cup (8–10 whole) strawberries, sliced

2 oz cream cheese, softened

2–3 tbsp chocolate hazelnut spread

2 tbsp butter, melted

¼ cup sugar

1 tsp cinnamon

Directions:

1. Preheat oven to 350°F and spray a standard muffin pan.
2. In a small bowl mix together cinnamon and sugar. In a separate bowl mix together cream cheese and chocolate hazelnut spread.
3. Make small marks in the dough to ensure uniform size. Start by making a mark in the middle, diving the dough into two parts. Continue to mark in the middle of each section until you have 64 marks.
4. Using a very sharp knife, slice the dough on the marks creating discs of dough. Use a rolling pin to roll each slice out thinner to create more of a surface to spread the cream cheese mixture.
5. Brush each slice with melted butter and sprinkle with cinnamon sugar.
6. Spread cream cheese mixture on all but 12 discs. Place several slices of strawberries on top of the cream cheese.
7. Stack 4 or 5 slices of dough and top with one of the 12 reserved discs so the stack starts and ends with dough. Cut the stack in half down the middle, creating 10–12 slices. Place the slices, cut side down, into the muffin cup. It should fit snuggly into the bottom of the cup.
8. Bake for 20–25 minutes, or until light golden brown.

TOASTED COCONUT AND CARAMEL COOKIE CUPS

There were moments during my recipe testing that I thought my roommate might strangle me. I made a total mess of the kitchen on more than one occasion. I think these coconut caramel cookie cups saved our relationship and my neck.

Pan: Mini 24-cup muffin pan

YOU WILL NEED:

Ingredients:
1 package sugar cookie dough
3 cups shredded coconut
1 (11oz) bag caramel bits

3 tbsp milk
⅛ tbsp salt
1 cup chocolate chips

Directions:

1. Preheat oven to 350°F and grease a mini muffin pan.

2. On a baking sheet, spread coconut in an even layer.

3. Toast at 350°F for 3 minutes. Give the coconut a stir and continue to bake for another 2 minutes, or until golden brown. Remove the oven and place aside.

4. Next, divide sugar cookie dough into 24 equal pieces and roll into balls. Place one ball of cookie dough into each muffin cup.

5. Bake for 10–12 minutes.

6. When the cookie cups are finished, remove from oven and allow to cool on a rack. The cups should start to sink in the middle. With the handle of a wooden spoon or your thumb when it has cooled enough, press the divot even further to create a well for the coconut filling.

7. In a microwave safe bowl, pour a bag of caramel bits, milk, and salt and microwave for 3 minutes, stopping and stirring every minute to prevent scorching.

8. When the caramel has melted, add coconut to it and stir very quickly to combine. Save a small amount of coconut if you wish to use it as a decorative topping.

9. Working very quickly and very carefully, use a small cookie scoop or tablespoon to create a ball of coconut and caramel. The mixture is very hot so be mindful not to burn your hands. Ball up the coconut caramel and place inside the cookie cups, pressing into the cup. Repeat with all the cookie cups.

10. Freeze for 30 minutes. Once the cookie cups have hardened, microwave the chocolate chips at 30-second intervals until melted. Place the rack over a baking sheet to catch any dripping chocolate.

11. Dip the tops of the frozen cups into the chocolate up the tops of the sugar cookie. Place on the cooling rack to allow the excess chocolate to drip off. Top chocolate with any leftover toasted coconut. Return the cups to the freezer for an additional 5 minutes.

12. When ready to eat, remove from the freezer and allow to come to room temperature before eating as they are very hard when frozen.

BITE-SIZED BACON PECAN PIE COOKIES

Y'all, there ain't nothing like letting a little Southern cookin' into your kitchen. These cookie cups are a quick and easy taste of a southern classic, pecan pie. Throw a little bacon and chocolate in there and folks won't be able to resist!

Pan: **Mini 24-cup muffin pan**

YOU WILL NEED:

Ingredients:

1 (16.5 oz) package of pre-made sugar cookie dough
1 cup pecan halves, chopped
⅔ cup dark chocolate chips

1 tsp dark corn syrup
¼ cup heavy whipping cream
4 slices of thick cut bacon (I used hickory smoked), cooked and chopped

Directions:

1. Preheat oven to 350°F and grease a 24-cup mini muffin pan.

2. Split the dough into 24 equal pieces, about 1 tablespoon a piece. Roll each piece into a ball and place into the cups of a greased mini muffin pan.

3. Press the dough into the bottom and up the side of each cup, leaving a shallow well in the middle of each cup.

4. Place one piece of bacon and several chocolate chips into each cup.

5. In a bowl, mix together chopped pecans, whipping cream, and corn syrup. Either pipe or pour the pecan mixture into each cookie cup.

6. Bake at 350°F for 20 minutes, or according to cookie package directions.

BUÑUELO CUPS WITH MINT STRAWBERRY SALSA

Sweet or savory, almost every country has a version of fried dough. In France it's beignets, in Italy they're called zeppoles, in East Africa they have mandazi, Chile has sopaipillas, Mexico has churros and in the States we have funnel cakes, doughnuts, elephants ears and Native American frybread, just to name a few. Buñuelos are a popular version of fried dough in many countries around the world including Argentina, Cuba, Spain, Greece and Morocco. Traditionally they are served around Christmas time and are covered in cinnamon and sugar. Sizes and shapes vary but they are often rolled into balls before frying. My version of buñuelos strays a bit from tradition. I opted for an easier flatter version, using flour tortillas as my base and baking them instead of frying. Still covered in plenty of cinnamon and sugar, these bowls make a great vessel for this fresh mint and strawberry salsa.

Pan: Standard 12-cup muffin pan

YOU WILL NEED:

Ingredients:
4 (8 in) flour tortillas
1 cup strawberries, diced
1 cup Granny Smith apples, diced
1 tsp fresh ginger, minced
Handful fresh mint, finely chopped

1 tbsp fresh lime juice
1 tbsp orange marmalade or jam
1 tbsp olive oil or melted butter
3 tbsp sugar
1–2 tsp cinnamon

Directions:

1. Preheat oven to 350°F and lightly spray down a 12-cup muffin pan.
2. Lightly butter both sides of each tortilla. Using the opening of a can or a biscuit cutter, cut circles into the tortilla. You should be able to get 3 circles for each large tortilla.
3. Pour cinnamon and sugar into a plastic container or plastic bag. Throw tortilla circles into the cinnamon sugar mixture and give it a shake. Coat both sides with cinnamon sugar.
4. Place one circle into each of the 12 muffin cups.
5. Bake at 350°F for 9–11 minutes.
6. While the tortillas are in the oven, mix the ingredients for the salsa together in a bowl.
7. Cover and place in the fridge while the tortillas cook and cool.
8. Once the tortillas have come out of the oven and cooled, fill them with strawberry salsa and serve. Garnish with mint.

WAFFLE CUP SUNDAES

Nothing says birthday party like ice cream sundaes! Try adding these waffle cups to your next ice cream social.

Pan: Jumbo 6-cup or standard 12-cup muffin pan

YOU WILL NEED:

Ingredients:
6–12 frozen waffles
1–2 cup(s) chocolate chips,
    for melting

Toppings:
Ice Cream
Sprinkles/Jimmies
Whipped Cream
Cherries
Walnuts/Almonds
Bananas

Directions:

1. Preheat the oven to 375°F and lightly spray the desired amount of muffin cups.
2. Defrost 6 waffles at a time in the microwave for 30–45 seconds.
3. Carefully press the waffle into each cup. Press gently into the sides. The top of the waffles will stick up over the edge of the cups. This is the part that will get covered in chocolate.
4. Bake for 12–14 minutes, or until nice and crisp.
5. In a microwave safe bowl, heat the chocolate chips at 30-second intervals until smooth. Dip the cooked waffle cups in the chocolate to coat the rim.
6. Add your desired toppings to the chocolate before it sets.

Party Time: *1.5 quarts of ice cream will fill 12 cups with a little extra leftover. You can use the empty muffin pan to display all the available toppings for guests to choose from.*

TEQUILA SUNRISE JELLO SHOOTERS!

Oh yes I did. Jello shots in the muffin pan. You can also use boxed jello to create your favorite shot flavor or color combination.

Pan: 2 standard 12-cup muffin pans

YOU WILL NEED:

Ingredients:
¾ cup grenadine
¼ cup water
4 envelopes gelatin

1½ cups orange juice
1½ cups gold tequila
Maraschino cherries

Directions:

1. Lightly spray a standard muffin pan and wipe out with paper towel. There should be just enough oil to help in removal but without affecting the taste.

2. In a small saucepan, combine grenadine and water. Sprinkle 1 package of gelatin on top and soak for 2 minutes.

3. Over low heat, whisk the mixture together for 5 minutes. All the gelatin should have fully dissolved. The mixture should not boil.

4. Divide the mixture among the cups, about a tablespoon per cup. Dry off and level the bottom of desired number of cherries. Place one in the center of each cup. Refrigerate for an hour.

5. In the same saucepan, pour in orange juice and sprinkle 3 packages of gelatin on top. Allow it to soak for 2 minutes.

6. Over low heat, whisk together orange juice and gelatin for 5 minutes until fully dissolved.

7. Remove saucepan from the heat and stir in tequila.

8. Allow the mixture to cool slightly before pouring it over the grenadine cherry layer.

9. Return the pan to the refrigerator. Chill for 4 hours or overnight until set.

Note: *If you want a gradient effect instead of two distinct layers in your tequila sunrise shot, then chill the grenadine layer for just 10 minutes before adding the orange layer. The orange layer will sink slowly to the bottom, forming a gradient effect instead of a layered effect.*

STRAWBERRY PRETZEL PIE BITES

These little bite-sized pies are everything. They are sweet, salty, creamy, and crunchy. I would suggest making two batches of these sweet and savory pies, one for you and your guests and one just for you. The very first time I made them they didn't make it beyond the refrigerator to the party. They are that good.

Pan: 2 mini 24-cup muffin pans

YOU WILL NEED:

Ingredients:

2 boxes of refrigerated pie crusts
1 cup crushed pretzels
6 tbsp butter, melted
¼ cup sugar
2 (8 oz) pkgs of cream cheese, softened
¼ cup sugar

1 pint heavy whipping cream
½ tsp vanilla
3 tbsp powdered sugar
½ lb frozen strawberries, thawed and thinly sliced
1 cup water, boiling
½ cup ice cubes
1 (6 oz) box of strawberry gelatin

Directions:

1. Preheat oven to 450°F and spray mini muffin pan, including the top of the pan.
2. Unroll all pie crusts onto a floured surface. Cut the pie dough into circles large enough to reach up the sides of the muffin cup. You may need to gather the scraps and roll out dough in order to get the desired number of circles. Place pie dough circles in the muffin cups and prick the dough with a fork to release air bubbles.
3. Place the pretzels in a zip top bag. Crush using a rolling pin or the bottom of a sturdy cup. Microwave butter until melted. To the bag of pretzels, add the melted butter and sugar. Give the bag a shake until the mixture is combined. Press a teaspoon or so of the pretzel mixture into the pie dough cups.
4. Bake for 10 to 12 minutes, or until golden brown. When finished, remove from oven and allow to cool completely.
5. In a stand mixer bowl fitted with whisk attachment, whip together heavy cream, vanilla, and powdered sugar on high. When the whipped cream has reached stiff peaks, after about 5 minutes, scoop out of the stand mixer bowl and place in another bowl.
6. In the same bowl of a stand mixer bowl now fitted with paddle attachment, beat together cream cheese and ¼ cup sugar. Carefully fold whipped cream into cream cheese mixture.
7. Pipe or spoon cheesecake filling on top of pretzels. Tap the tray on the counter to ensure the filling moves to the bottom. Place a layer of 2 or 3 strawberry slices on top of the filling.
8. In a spouted bowl, mix together boiling water with gelatin. Add ice cubes and stir until gelatin is dissolved. Pour gelatin over strawberry slices. Make sure to cover the entire top. Don't worry about overfilling.
9. Refrigerate the tray for 8 hours or overnight.

TIRAMISU PUDDING IN CHOCOLATE CUPS

These little chocolate cups are so fun to make and great for entertaining. If tiramisu isn't your thing, try filling these cups with berries and cream. So simple yet very impressive.

Pan: **Standard 12-cup silicone muffin pan**

Ingredients:

1 (12 oz) bag chocolate chips

1 cup heavy cream

¼ sugar

1 cup mascarpone or ricotta

1 tbsp unsweetened cocoa

1 tbsp coffee flavored liquor or irish cream

1 tsp instant espresso granules

Vanilla wafers, crumbled

Directions:

1. In a microwave safe bowl, melt chocolate in the microwave for about a minute and a half. Stop and stir every 30 seconds to prevent scorching. Allow to cool slightly. The cooler the chocolate is, the better it will adhere to the mold.

2. Pour a small amount of chocolate into either the silicone muffin pan or paper cups. Start by spreading the chocolate along the bottom of the cup. Then, using a small amount from the bowl, spread the chocolate up the sides of the cup. A paintbrush or the back of a spoon both work well for this application.

3. Be liberal with the chocolate. The thicker the base, the easier it will be to remove and will help prevent cracking. To ensure a thick layer, especially if the treats will be sitting out, allow the first layer of chocolate to set in the fridge for 5 minutes. Then remove from fridge and paint on a second layer of chocolate all around the cup.

4. Allow the cups to set in the refrigerator for an hour or more. Remove from the refrigerator when you are ready to fill.

5. While the chocolate sets, prepare tiramisu filling.

6. In a food processor fitted with a whipping attachment, whip together heavy cream and sugar until it forms stiff peaks. Scoop out of the food processor and place in a bowl.

7. In the same food processor vessel, combine mascarpone, cocoa, Kahlua, and instant espresso. Combine well. Return whipped cream to the food processor bowl and fold until there are no streaks.

8. Carefully remove chocolate bowls from the muffin pan. Add the crumbled vanilla wafers and spoon the tiramisu mixture into the chocolate bowl. Serve chilled.

CHOCOLATY CHEX BITES

This is a simple snack, perfect for adding to school lunches or taking on a short hike.

Pan: 2 standard 12-cup muffin pans, in silicone or metal

YOU WILL NEED:

Ingredients:

4 cups of Chex, Whole Wheat, Rice, or Corn
1 ½ cups pretzels, bite sized or crushed
1 cup mixed nuts or peanuts
1 (8 oz) bag Heath toffee bits

¼ cup butter, melted
1 tsp vanilla extract
1 cup creamy peanut butter
1 cup corn syrup
1 cup brown sugar
3 cups dark chocolate chips

Directions:

1. Grease a muffin pan or use a silicone muffin pan.

2. In a large bowl combine chex, pretzels, toffee bits, and nuts.

3. In a small bowl stir together butter and vanilla. Pour butter mixture over chex and toss with your hands until well coated.

4. In a sauce pan over medium heat, combine peanut butter, corn syrup, and brown sugar. Cook until the mixture begins to boil around the edges. Stir continuously so as to not burn the mixture. Remove the pan from heat and pour on top of the chex mix.

5. Gently stir the chex mixture around with a rubber spatula. Scoop the mixture into the cups of the muffin pan.

6. Microwave chocolate chips in a bowl for 2 minutes, stopping to stir every 30 seconds or so until fully melted. Spoon or pour chocolate over the tops of the chex bites.

7. Place tray in the refrigerator for an hour to set. When ready to serve, use a knife to pop the bites out of the muffin pan.

CARAMEL FILLED
CINNAMON SUGAR PRETZEL BUNS

I am not a big dessert person. I admit it. I prefer salty treats to sweets but I love these cinnamon sugar pretzel buns. The surprise of having caramel in the middle is just enough sweet for me.

Pan: Mini 24-cup muffin pan

YOU WILL NEED:

Ingredients:

1 ½ cups warm (105–110°F) water
1 tbsp granulated sugar
1 packet active dry yeast
4 ½ cups AP flour
2 tsp kosher salt
4 tbsp unsalted butter, melted

10 cups or 3 quarts of water
⅔ cup baking soda
Cinnamon
Sugar
Caramel bits
1 egg yolk
1 tbsp water
Kosher or sea salt

Directions:

1. Preheat oven to 400°F.
2. Combine water, sugar, and yeast in the bowl of a stand mixer; let sit 5 minutes until foamy.
3. Add flour, salt and butter; stir to combine. Using a dough hook, knead dough on medium speed 5 minutes until smooth, elastic, and slightly tacky (alternatively, you can turn the dough out onto a lightly floured surface and knead by hand 10 minutes).
4. Shape dough into a ball and place in a large, lightly greased bowl. Cover with lightly greased plastic wrap and let rise in a warm place for 1 hour until doubled.
5. When dough is nearly doubled, combine water and baking soda in a large stockpot. Bring to a boil.
6. Punch down dough. Split the dough, you'll only need half for this recipe. Pinch off small piece of dough, just smaller than a ping pong ball. Flatten each piece of dough in your hand. In the center place 3 or 4 small caramel bits. Wrap the dough around the caramel. Repeat this until all the dough is used.
7. Place about 4–5 bites at a time in the boiling water bath; boil 30 seconds. Using a slotted spoon, remove bites and place in the wells of the muffin pan. Repeat with remaining pies.
8. Whisk together egg and water to create a wash. Lightly brush tops of pies with egg wash. In a small bowl combine cinnamon and sugar. Generously sprinkle cinnamon sugar over the tops. Bake 12 to 14 minutes until golden brown and puffed. Cool slightly on a cooling rack before serving.

HOW TO HOST
A MAC AND CHEESE BAR

Now that you have popped the mac and cheese bites in the oven, it is time to set up your spread!

There are no limits for what tastes good on top of cheesy noodles. You can serve up whatever you have on hand or stick to the theme of the party. Try using ingredients that compliment the rest of the fare. The possibilities are endless.

Here are some ideas for toppings:

Meat – *bacon bits, diced ham, grilled slices of chicken, prosciutto, sliced steak, lump crab meat, ground sausage, diced Andouille, chopped salami, shredded pork, shrimp, chopped lobster, ground meat, shredded rotisserie chicken, chorizo, diced hot dogs*

Vegetables – *cherry tomatoes, sautéed mushrooms, green onions, caramelized onions, green chilies, chipotle peppers in adobo, spinach, jalapenos, roasted garlic, peas, banana peppers, chopped bell peppers, artichoke hearts, sun-dried tomatoes*

Seasoning and Herbs – *Cajun seasonings, chili powder, Spanish paprika, basil, onion powder, parsley, taco seasonings, seasoning salt, cilantro*

Special Touches – *buffalo sauce, sour cream, goat cheese, lime wedges, sriracha, walnuts, avocado, Gorgonzola crumbles, ranch, olives, potato chips, cubed cream cheese, ricotta*

Once you've narrowed down your toppings, the muffin pan can be used to display them. How's that for multi-purpose?! You can use the flat top of the muffin pan to label the toppings. Place the tray next to the mac and cheese bites along with forks and napkins.

It could also be fun to offer your guests some suggestions for topping combinations. Maybe a house specialty, a combo created for a guest of honor, a mixture befitting the birthday boy or girl, etc. If you would like some ideas, why not try these flavor combinations:

Flashback
hot dog and potato chips . . . and ketchup,
if you insist.

Bistro
caramelized onion, bacon bits, goat cheese

Buffalo
rotisserie chicken, crumbled gorgonzola and green onions, top with buffalo sauce

Philly
sliced steak, bell peppers, sautéed mushrooms

Fiesta
chorizo, green chilies, cilantro, squeeze of lime

Bourbon Street
Andouille sausage, shrimp, peas, Cajun seasoning

There you go. The best part of the mac and cheese bar is that it runs itself. All you have to do is sit back, watch your friends and family get creative and enjoy.

ACKNOWLEDGMENTS

I can't say thank you enough to the people who have helped me along this cookbook journey. To my parents, Tony and Marie, thank you for being so supportive of this project. I really could not have done it without your help. You believed in me, even on those days when I didn't believe in myself. You never doubted I would succeed and for that I am truly grateful. I love you.

To my brother and sister, Joey and Becky, you are my favorites. I am so proud of you both. Thanks for always making me laugh.

To my best friend, Nadia, thank you for answering my frantic phone calls and restoring my confidence in myself. You said I could do it so I knew I could. I am so lucky to have your love and support.

To my Bright Horizons family, a.k.a. The Sisterhood of the Traveling Cat Pants, thank you for being my official taste testers. I really appreciate your feedback, compliments, and tips. Thanks for the advice, the endless amounts of patience, the time off, the extra hours, the rides to and from work, and the kindness you've always shown. I am so happy to spend my days working along side such a fantastic team.

Thank you to the HaHa Sisterhood for being an amazing extended family. You have taught me so much about food, photography, and how to live a full and happy life.

To my roommate, thanks for letting me leave dirty dishes in the sink. Your patience is really appreciated.

To my friends and family who I have not named, thank you thank you THANK YOU! Many of you offered to clean dishes, test recipes, help cook, gave ideas, lent cookbooks, lent kitchen space or just took me out when I needed a break. You all hold a very special place in my heart. Emily, Katie, and Kelly, I can't tell you how much I appreciate your words of encouragement while I nervously sent my first draft all the way from Tanzania to New York. Thank you for helping me keep my cool when all I wanted to do was panic. You guys are the best cheerleaders and travel partners anyone could ask for.

A big thanks to Joey Sverchek for believing in me. I would not be writing this book if it weren't for you.

And to my editor, Kristin Kulsavage at Skyhorse Publishing, for giving me this opportunity to show off my skills. Thank you for your advice and patience. You took a chance on me and had faith in my abilities. That is the biggest compliment I could ever receive. You have been wonderful.